Democracy Against Liberalism

Democracy Against Liberalism

Its Rise and Fall

Aviezer Tucker

polity

First published in 2020 by Polity Press

Polity Press
65 Bridge Street
Cambridge CB2 1UR, UK

Polity Press
101 Station Landing
Suite 300
Medford, MA 02155, USA

ISBN-13: 978-1-5095-4120-1 (hardback)
ISBN-13: 978-1-5095-4121-8 (paperback)

A catalogue record for this book is available from the British Library.

Typeset in 11 on 13pt Sabon
by Fakenham Prepress Solutions, Fakenham, Norfolk NR21 8NL
Printed and bound in Great Britain by TJ International Limited

For further information on Polity, visit our website:
politybooks.com

Contents

1

What's Your Problem? Illiberalism, Populism, Authoritarianism

We have been living in interesting times recently, as the apocryphal Chinese curse goes. A political apocalypse seems to follow a cascade of calamities, rolling waves of economic recessions and downturns, social discontents, and political upheavals that have reinforced each other since 2008. This "return of history" threatens to replace liberal democracy with illiberal populism.

Populist neo-illiberalism has generated engaged interest and earnest confusion in equal measures. The verb "to happen," especially in the indefinite passive voice has become the key political verb. Politicians, commentators, and social scientists reacted as if a meteor had stricken the political planet. Nobody quite understood what hit them. Nobody was responsible, but everybody has become anxious. A telling example is Hillary Clinton's electoral self-postmortem autopsy, entitled *What Happened?* Madeleine Albright in a book entitled *Fascism: A Warning* (2018) replied: "Trump happened." Things happen, unfortunate events "befall," when there is no agency and no responsibility. Denial of responsibility assumes historical inevitability; it happened because it had to happen and nothing anybody could have done would have changed that. Alternatively, at the cost of accepting responsibility, it is possible to regain agency and accept that things could have been different, history could have taken a different course, had some people made better choices.

The current reversal in the fortunes of liberalism, the onset of populist-driven neo-illiberalism that gradually deconstructs institutional checks and balances has taken place in a dazzlingly broad scope of countries of entirely different histories and political cultures. It started in weakly liberal post-totalitarian democracies when populist illiberals won democratic elections in Hungary and Poland, and proceeded gradually to dismantle feeble liberal institutions. In Hungary, illiberalism progressed sufficiently to subvert free and fair elections and establish an authoritarian, illiberal, populist regime with unfair elections, where gerrymandered districting is designed to transmute a large minority or a small majority of the votes into an absolute special majority in the parliament that can revise the constitution at will, change the rules of the political game as it proceeds to guarantee the winner. The coronavirus pandemic crisis seems to have given the regime the final excuse to give even democracy the *coup-de-grâce* to become fully authoritarian.

Over the same period, Netanyahu's Likud government in Israel, a country with much older, stronger, and better entrenched liberal institutions, has become increasingly illiberal, attacking and attempting to take over the judiciary, the media, the civil service, educated elites, independent artists, and the Ombudsman, while attempting with decreasing success to suppress the votes of Israeli Arabs. In 2016, it became obvious that populist-illiberalism is not confined to Europe's Eastern and Southern margins, when Donald Trump won the US presidential elections in one of the oldest continuously existing liberal democracies, and proceeded to attack the ultra-strong and well-entrenched US liberal institutions, the judiciary, the security services, the media, the Central Bank, and so on, while attempting to dismantle checks and balances within the administration and to by-pass the legislative branch of government.

Populist neo-illiberal parties have not only entered parliaments, but also coalition governments in Europe, a phenomenon that used to be confined to post-Nazi Austria. India, the largest democracy that maintained many liberal institutions in the British tradition has also turned illiberal, following the election of the Bharatiya Janata Party (BJP). It attempts to disenfranchise and perhaps even deport some of its 200 million Moslem citizens through a new citizenship law. Finally, Brazil, a post-authoritarian country, also seems to have gone down the populist neo-illiberal path, with the 2019 election of Bolsonaro as president. This puzzling apparent absence of historical path dependency calls for an explanation.

Some pundits with professional or amateur interest in political theory have dusted off old, off the shelf concepts, and searched the inventories of political history for more or less appropriate analogies. Others floated new fuzzy conceptual balloons that quickly deflated from over-inflation. Other conceptual lead balloons were so overloaded with complex details that they failed to lift off the ground with more than a single example.

Conceptual "family" relations proved dysfunctional: Some authoritarian regimes are illiberal, and some illiberals are populist, and so it is possible to generate a concept of all three and call it either populist, or illiberal, or authoritarian. But political history is long and complex. Some authoritarian regimes were liberal. Even more disorienting are democratic regimes that were populist and liberal, not to mention democracies that were sometimes technocratic and illiberal. Political conceptualization by free association creates unmanageable amalgamations of historically contingent concepts. It is too easy to slide from populism to illiberalism and then to authoritarianism, not just politically, but also conceptually.

The problem is not in the political stars but in ourselves, in the expectation that the political world would align itself neatly in binary choices between good and evil, democracy and authoritarianism, liberalism and illiberalism, and the equally simplistic expectation that all the good and bad types should neatly align themselves on the same side: liberal democracy against illiberal populist authoritarians. As Mounk (2018) noted, political understanding should commence with the realization that the coupling of liberalism and democracy was a historical coincidence. Liberalism and democracy are quite independent of each other, though we have come to call the liberal–democratic coincidence, simply democracy (Sartori 1987).

A good-versus-evil Manichean, binary and unidimensional, political worldview has been reinforced since the end of the Second World War, through the Cold War. It divided the world between the democratic liberal light and the authoritarian forces of darkness. Light won over darkness in 1989–1991, and that was supposed to be the end. Liberal democracy should have been the curtain call of history. But political regimes have been multi-dimensional. Their differences are discrete yet continuous. The world is full of shades of grey, though some shades of grey are considerably closer to black or white than others.

President Trump is exceedingly adept at getting under the skin of people who dislike him, to become the center of attention. Too many scholars are happy to oblige. Many books in the democratic apocalypse genre, especially those originating from the United States, are obsessed with understanding "Trump" and how anybody could have voted for him. I try a different approach, I want to understand neo-illiberalism by "decentering" Trump from a historical comparative perspective, to pigeonhole him and his ilk in their proper comparative political-historical contexts.

This book understands and explains *neo-illiberal democracy* theoretically and historically. It distinguishes the contemporary episode of illiberal democracy from its previous historical incarnations. The book examines the possible causes of neo-illiberal democracy and predicts its instability. I argue that the political travails of the second decade of the twenty-first century were evitable. Finally, I propose new policies to preempt comparable crises of populist illiberalism in the future by preempting political passions, strengthening institutions, and tinkering with a few political mechanisms. If successful, these measures will result in new liberalism without nostalgia

Perhaps if theorists wish to see neo-illiberal populist democracy killed, they'd better dissect it first. Distinct political concepts should be clear, unambiguous, and above all, simple! Theorists need to weed out conceptually inessential or historically accidental properties. Only necessary minimal properties that distinguish regime types should be left in the end. Simplicity cuts through the conceptual fog and may even clear the political air.

Let's start with "bikini" concepts that cover the bare minimum and are distinct. I introduce three *discrete* and *continuous* rather than *binary* political dimensions that stretch between opposing poles. The following three dimensions are sufficient and necessary for understanding the political crises that followed 2008:

Democracy |-------------------------------| Authoritarianism
Liberalism |-------------------------------| Absolutism
                                                                   (Illiberalism)
Technocracy |-------------------------------| Populism

Though many associate the above left and right poles with each other to form unified Manichean good-versus-evil concepts (liberal technocratic democracy versus populist absolute authoritarianism), historically, these correlations were uncommon. I use familiar terms, democracy and authoritarianism, liberalism and absolutism, populism and technocracy in simpler and more limited, "bikini," senses than is usual in political theory. I seek greater precision than in "fluid" journalistic ordinary language where terms flow into each other to create murky conceptual puddles.

Democracy vs. Authoritarianism

Democracy is often over-extended to include liberal institutional and cultural prerequisites. Democracy, civil rights, and the rule of law may well reinforce each other, but most democracies have not been liberal. If democracies that are not liberal and far from ideal in excluding resident aliens, or slaves, or the poor, or women, or have authoritarian elements, are excluded from the pure and pious democratic ideal, democracy becomes a utopian normative ideal that may not fit any historical regime and cannot explain the political world. Many democracies, including all the ancient ones, were surely more distant from the authoritarian pole than the democratic ideal pole, though none was liberal or respected rights. I use a minimal measure of democracy as the *degree to which the government represents the citizens' political choices in free and fair elections.* On one pole there are authoritarian regimes that do not represent their citizens, while on the other pole there is pure proportional representation without a threshold, where all the citizens and residents vote. Hybrid authoritarian–democratic regimes that combine authoritarian features with limited political competition and unfair elections are in the middle (Levitsky and Way 2010). Closer still to the authoritarian pole are authoritarian regimes that allow limited representative elections, though the representative bodies do not govern, but represent or advise. *Authoritarian* regimes, by contrast, do not *represent* the political choices of their subjects, even when they *reflect* them. Even when the policies of an authoritarian regime happen to agree with what its subjects would have preferred had they been given the choice, they are not given the choice, and the regime does not represent them. Authoritarian regimes can be more or less popular, but they are not *accountable* to their subjects.

Liberalism vs. Absolutism

I use *liberalism* as a constitutional institutional and social structure that checks and limits the size, scope, and reach of government. Liberalism can co-exist with democratic, authoritarian, and other regimes, but not with totalitarianism that can accept no institutional or legal limits. In modern societies, liberalism is manifest in the rule of law enforced by independent branches of government, such as the judiciary. Some of these institutions guarantee rights. Without institutions, rights are ideals and ideologies, not political reality, "nonsense upon stilts" as Jeremy Bentham put it. *Absolutism* is the opposite of liberalism. It eschews checks or balances on the scope, size, or power of government. Absolutism can be authoritarian as well as democratic.

Liberalism developed originally to submit monarchs to laws that codified traditional and not so traditional rights, as interpreted by independent judges. Absolutist governments could and did grant *privileges* and sufferance to minorities and civil society, but they could rescind them at will. The universality of the rule of law protected the rights of minorities and the autonomy of civil society. The state's size, powers, and capacities grew with the expansion and professionalization of state bureaucracy and following technological advances. It has become necessary, then, to increase the number and strength of liberal institutions to preserve the balance between the powers of the state and society. The division between the three branches of government became insufficient. Other independent institutions accumulated, including institutional religion, the free and independent media, the education system, and the Central Bank. These institutions may be financed by the government as long as they maintain their independence. The modern liberal state is further bound by a web of international treaties and agreements that are adjudicated and implemented by international liberal institutions such as the World Bank, the International Monetary Fund, the International Trade Agreement, and the European Union.

The liberal to absolutist dimension is continuous. Even absolute monarchies were not entirely unencumbered by institutions. When the French monarchy needed to increase taxation, it had to call the estates, thereby triggering the French Revolution. The independence of central banks is historically recent and resulted from the populist temptation of democratic governments to push interest rates too low for too long and generate hyper-inflation. Other institutions, like the political party, may limit the power of government by forcing it to use the party's mediation to connect with supporters. Absolutist governments prefer unmediated personalized relationships with unorganized and unstructured followers. Successful ancient demagogues, tribunes of the plebs, and dictators had such a direct relation with masses and mobs.

Absolutism describes better the opposite pole to liberalism than *illiberalism* because it has been in use and debated for centuries. However, in the contemporary political context, *illiberalism* has become the entrenched dominant term in use, at least since Fareed Zakaria (2003) popularized the term "illiberal democracy," and Hungary's prime minister Viktor Orbán dusted it off for his own needs. In this book I use *illiberalism* and *absolutism* interchangeably. I use *neo-illiberalism*, the main topic of this book, in contemporary contexts, and *absolutism* when writing about history, to emphasize that this is a new incarnation of an old type of regime.

Populism vs. Technocracy

Standard contemporary theories of populism associate it with social movements that emphasize the struggle of homogeneous "people" versus perfidious "elites." (Canovan 2005; Norris and Inglehart 2019). Populism in the United States resulted partly from resentment against elite and expert blunders in initiating and conducting the Iraq War and in bringing about, not preempting, and failing to quickly end the 2008–2009 Great Recession to restore the prior trajectory of the economy. Subsidizing the managerial class, and bailing out the banks that caused the mess in the first place, added insult to injury. In this respect, it may be argued that George W. Bush's administration successfully achieved a regime change, though not the one intended and not in the country targeted.

This standard characterization is too broad. It would consider populist too many political episodes that are clearly not populist. It would also leave out much of contemporary populism. Representations of political struggles as those of the "people" in the depths of subterranean society against stratospheric elites have been characteristic of rebels, religious reform movements, socialists, anti-colonialists, and nationalist struggles in multi-national empires. Anti-intellectuals who resent better educated, artistically sensitive, and abstract-minded elites include human resources departments of major corporations and investment bankers, who resent academic "experimentation." Since elites are by definition fewer than "ordinary people," and their privileges or perceived privileges often generate some resentment, it usually makes good democratic politics to attack them. Parties that represented the interests of the poor, the rural, or the more religious, attempted to harness resentments against the wealthy, urban, and secular, without being "populist." Socialist, small holders, and Christian parties are often not populist. Mere anti-elitist rhetoric is insufficiently distinctive of populism.

Anti-elitist concepts of populism are also too narrow because they exclude obviously populist movements that adore elite plutocrats (or apparent plutocrats) such as Berlusconi in Italy, Babiš in the Czech Republic, and Trump in the United States. Most ancient populist demagogues in Greece and Rome were scions of famous and old political families. Some contemporary populists respect and even admire wealthy elites and celebrities like the Italian populist leader Pepe Grillo and, of course, Trump. Trump's fear of divulging his tax returns probably reflects status anxiety. He fears losing the respect and adoration of his followers should they realize that he is not much richer than they are. Contemporary populists do not necessarily resent professional politicians. Some populist leaders had been professional mainstream center-right or center-left politicians before adopting populist style and politics; for example, Hungary's prime minister Orbán, the Czech president Zeman, and Israel's prime minister Netanyahu. Though India's Modi had modest caste origins, he was also a professional politician, the chief minister of Gujarat for over a decade, and his policies have been distinctly favorable to the upper castes. Brazil's Bolsonaro was a professional politician for decades after being a military officer in a country with a traditionally political and authoritarian military. The Polish populist leader Kaczyński was both a celebrity actor and a professional politician. By contrast, virtually all the totalitarian leaders, Mussolini, Hitler, Lenin, Stalin, Mao, and their close associates, had no elite background of any kind.

The political etymology of the term "populist" goes back to the late Roman Republic (133–27 BCE), when conflicts between the *Optimates* and *Populares* tore it apart in civil wars. Both groups were of elite Roman families, but the weaker clique sought popular support in its struggle with the stronger party that controlled the Roman Senate. The struggle was not so much between the people and the elites as between factions within the elite, some of whom did not shy away from attempting to use common people to support them. In response, the *Optimates* accused the *Populares* of demagoguery, the emotional manipulation of the political passions of the masses.

At least since Plato, upper-class authors and orators have attempted to associate the passions exclusively with the lower classes. Conversely, they associated self-control and reason with the upper classes. The oligarchic conclusion is obvious and fully developed in Plato's political philosophy: An elite moved by reason rather than passion should rule, if not enslave, people who cannot rule their own passions. Democracy, the rule of common people who cannot control their passions and subdue them to reason leads to the politics of the passions, demagoguery, and eventually self-destruction.

Elite propaganda aside, the ancient Greek and Roman elites were just as likely as the lower classes to succumb to passions, both political and personal. Passions for social domination, economic rapaciousness, and arrogant condescension begot resentment and class warfare. The difference between the ancient classes was not marked by reason versus passion, but by different kinds of passions, different tastes for self-destructiveness, like the difference between single malt whiskey thrice distilled and industrial alcohol: consumed in sufficient quantities, they both kill, though at different price ranges and levels of smoothness. Elite and popular populisms fed on each other and led to mutual destruction in civil wars, the end of the republic.

I adopt the core of the ancient concept of populism as the politics of passions, while rejecting its class bias, the exclusive association of the passions with lower classes. I propose to interpret populism, ancient and contemporary, as the rule of *political passions*. I maintain the ancient association of populism with passions and their manipulation by demagogues, but drop the class bias that associated populism exclusively with the politics of bread and circuses in Rome or beer and sausages in Marx's view of the politics of the undisciplined poor, the *Lumpenproletariat*.

The eighteenth-century "moralists" introduced a useful Greek-inspired tripartite division of motivations between *passions*, *interests*, and *reason*. Contemporary political theorists like Jon Elster used this terminology to explain politics and liberal constitutions. Framers of such constitutions foresaw circumstances when politicians and voters would be compelled by passions to act against their interests. They enacted constitutions that constrain passionate choices, much as a sober recovering alcoholic may give the keys to the liquor cabinet to a trusted friend, with the instruction not to open it, irrespective of what the alcoholic may say in the future. Liberal institutions like the independent judiciary and central bank act as that trusted friend, to constrain political passions. *Neo-illiberalism* lifts such constraints to permit the politics of passions, populism.

The distinctions between passions, interests, and reason do not have to presume value judgments about which motivations are "legitimate" or "rational" and which are not. When the realization of passions comes at the expense of most other life projects, the passions are clearly and distinctly self-destructive. For example, irrespective of which life projects and goals jealous spouses may have, if they commit murder in jealous rage, whatever else they may have wished for, the rest of their lives will become impossible. Similarly, some economic policies give precedence to economic growth and social mobility, while others prefer economic equality and social cohesion. But populist policies, as in Venezuela, destroy the economy to an extent that growth and equality, mobility and cohesion, all become impossible.

Not all passions are sufficiently extreme to be assuredly self-destructive. Some passions lead the people they motivate to take extreme risks, thereby increasing the probability, rather than certainty, of self-destruction. Political passionate recklessness may pay off when the populists who lead it are lucky. They may come to believe themselves invincible, smart, or empowered by their passions, until luck runs out.

Other passions come at the expense of interests that, upon reflection and consideration, people would give precedence to. As La Bruyere (quoted in Elster 1999, 337) put it: "Nothing is easier for passion than to overcome reason, but the greatest triumph is to conquer a man's own interest." For example, anger has led people in history to burn down their own neighborhoods. They lived another day, but made themselves homeless. States have overreacted to provocations, built lavish dysfunctional buildings, and paid for the rescue of whales caught in ice, when the same resources could have been allocated for other purposes (hospitals, orphanages etc.) that both government and people, upon reflection, would have recognized as more important. Populists find challenging postponement of gratification to maximize satisfaction, giving precedence to some motivations over others, and recognizing that scarcity of resources forces choices between motivations.

Populists tend to miss what Harry Frankfurte (1988, 11–25) called second-order *volitions,* a will to determine their own passions. Populists accept all their passions and do not recognize contradictions between the passions; the constraints that satisfying some imposes on satisfying others. Demagogue may enflame and manipulate passions, but cannot control them and would not try. Populist leaders must promise immediate gratification in the form of simple policy solutions that they may misrepresent as having no undesirable consequences. They cannot acknowledge the complexity of the world (Mounk 2018, 36–39). When populist leaders cannot gratify, they divert attention to something else. Populist passions demand policies that are incompatible and undermine each other. They necessitate more policies to correct those contradictions, and so on. This is most obvious in macro-economic policies that want to improve public services, reduce taxes, and keep inflation and the national debt down; or keep high levels of transfer payments from the young to the old, with low birth rates, and strict restrictions on immigration of young workers, as in Japan. Populist policies, as distinct from populist rhetoric or expressions of passion, eventually consume themselves in self-destructive bonfire of passions.

Populist passions can be powerful enough to affect the *beliefs* of their adherents. Beliefs become narrative representations of passions, rather than probable results of reliable processes of inference from evidence. For example, if populists hate or fear somebody, they come to believe that they must have committed horrible crimes. Since the passions precede the stories told to represent them, evidence cannot convince or dissuade the passions. For example, fear and hate may cause populists to believe that immigrants commit higher rates of crimes than natives; while continuously ignoring the glaring evidence to the contrary. Vice versa, American populists ignore the fact that almost all the mass shootings in the United States have been committed by native white males because there is no corresponding passion to this belief.

Whether or not populist leaders actually possess the passions they manipulate or rather use the passions of others to further their own interests, is neither clear nor important. "Great orators are those who somehow manage to have it both ways, to enjoy the benefits of sincerity and those of misrepresentation. Their emotions belong to ... the gray area between transmutation and misrepresentation; they are neither fully genuine nor entirely feigned" (Elster 1999, 390). For example, pluto-crats whose businesses are becoming uncompetitive have an interest in protectionism and overregulation as well as in misrepresenting their protectionist interests as xenophobic passions shared with many others with no such interests. Likewise, employers who rely on cheap immigrant labor have an interest in presenting themselves as xenophobes who promote immigration restrictions because it strengthens their bargaining position with the undocumented workers they employ, while presenting themselves as ideologically above suspicions of employing illegal immigrants.

No person or state can always be entirely in control of their passions. There are degrees of populism, as the politics of the passions, just as there are degrees of democracy and liberalism. The exact borderline between populist and not so populist systems that have some populist aspects can be disputed, just like the borderline between democracy and authoritarianism and liberalism and absolutism. The extreme cases are obvious, while the exact classification of intermediate cases may be ambiguous. Moderate levels of populism can be sustainable. For example, some expensive penal policies are neither in the interest of victims nor of reforming perpetrators, but satisfy passions for revenge and retribution. Passionate politics have costs and unintended consequences, but the political system may be able to pay them without becoming insolvent. The transition from systems that have some populist aspects to populism proper is gradual, resembling a live frog slowly and gradually boiling into a soup.

Populism as the politics of the passions is important for understanding *neo-illiberalism*, the topic of this book, because liberal constitutions and institutions were designed and constructed often to constrain and even block the political expressions of passions and absolutist governments. Liberalism gets in the way of much of populism. Varieties of populism that find themselves in conflict with constitutions and institutions like the independent judiciary can make common cause with absolutists or illiberals who are not necessarily populist but want the liberal institutions out of their way so they can exercise absolute political power.

The contemporary alliance between illiberals (or absolutists) and populists is an alliance of convenience and not of conviction. To the extent that the illiberal leaders understand and act on their interests, they know they cannot enact policies that accord with populist passions or bring their own demise. Orbán cannot start a war with Romania to restore Hungary to its pre-Trianon Treaty size. Trump cannot block most trade with China and Mexico. Nobody can borrow to finance public services without eventually raising more money from taxes. The populist neo-illiberal trick then is to manipulate the passions; make symbolic gestures like building useless walls on the border of Mexico and sending soldiers to protect the country from migrants that do not exist in East Europe, while using bombastic language. For example, Poland has at once one of the most liberal non-populist immigration policies in Europe with millions of immigrants from outside the EU (mostly from Ukraine), while its leaders have some of the most anti-immigration and anti-EU rhetoric in Europe. When all else fails, the illiberals can distract passion with passion, like a new object of fear or hatred. Populist crowds have many passions that they do not fully understand and express, so the demagogue can trigger and manipulate them.

The populists and neo-illiberals have a common goal of dismantling liberal institutions. But they do not share common interests. Populist illiberal leaders have no interest in acting on the populist passions that would lead to their self-destruction. They have an interest in obtaining and maintaining absolute power. This interest in absolute power is shared by all the neo-illiberal politicians, though it is not exclusive to them. Once they have such power, many, though not all, will further use it for personal enrichment and corruption, which is against the interests of their populist supporters. The dilemma of populist illiberals in power is that the stronger they express the populist passions, the more support and legitimacy they receive in their confrontation with liberal institutions. Yet, the more they actually act on those passions, the greater is the risk that the regime would collapse under the pressure of its own passions. The populist illiberals are constrained by reality from acting on much of their rhetoric. Consequently they increase the volume of the rhetoric and provoke. Small populist policies can generate a lot of noise but little damage. For example, provoking liberals by being rude and trampling on norms of political respect, or making symbolic gestures such as building symbolic borders, putting poor immigrant children in cages (morally abhorrent but politically inconsequential), and prohibiting the migration of people from countries that send few high-net-worth immigrants, are populist policies that create much more noise than actual political damage. Should illiberal populists start acting on their rhetoric, as in classical ancient absolute democracies, populist self-destruction will follow.

The opposite political pole to populism is technocracy, the rule of experts. Experts should represent instrumental rationality in the service of interests. Since Plato, the technocratic ideal has been for the rulers to be knowledgeable experts. Plato had a non-specialized, holistic, concept of knowledge and political expertise. He "appointed" philosophers to run his utopian technocracy. Contemporary notions of expertise prefer applied specialists to theoreticians. Mounk (2018) documented the growth of technocracy since the 1930s, including liberal bureaucracies exempted from democratic elections, such as quasi-non-governmental organizations that are financed by the state but are not controlled by its representative bodies. Technocracies do not have to be liberal; they can serve absolutist states, as well as authoritarian or democratic governments. Indeed, all modern monarchies and dictatorship had to use at least some technocrats.

Plato identified in his *Republic* two related problems with technocracies. When self-proclaimed experts disagree, as they often do, there is no higher authority to decide who the real experts are, who has knowledge and who has mere opinion. Experts also have group and personal interests that may bias their judgments. A technocratic class may mistake its own self-interest or even, perish the thought, its passions, for expert analysis. Indeed, Plato's own political philosophy may be interpreted in such terms. Technocrats are just as corruptible as everybody else both as individuals with interests, and as a class that has shared common interests in protecting its privileges.

Since experts as a class cannot be trusted to act more impartially than anybody else, liberal constitutions place them in institutions that should supervise and compete with each other. The increase in the power and complexity of the state has required a commensurable growth in technocratic liberal institutions that balance each other like the Central Bank, the BBC, and the Ombudsman, and so on, to check the power of the technocratic state. That mutual growth is not contradictory but necessary, the bigger the state is, the more necessary it is to curb its powers. It is impossible for *modern* states to function with no technocratic expertise and assistance. Even if policy ends are dictated by the passions, populist politicians need a technocratic bureaucracy to devise means to try to realize them. The horrors of twentieth-century totalitarianism and authoritarianism resulted from the efficient use of technocrats to implement passionate politics.

Eight Regimes

The eight possible combinations of the three continuous pairs of ideal types (Populist vs. Technocratic; Liberal vs. Absolutist; and Democratic vs. Authoritarian) can be represented in a table with eight cells, as below.

These eight regime types are ideal. There are many intermediary forms between the extreme poles. For example, in the modern world, even populist governments must rely on some technocratic expertise. Democratic politicians, even in liberal technocracies sometimes indulge in manipulating popular passions. But these are useful signposts for demarcation and orientation in the vast political landscape. To elaborate a bit on these eight forms before concentrating on populist illiberal democracy:

Authoritarian absolutism, populist or *technocratic,* is a simple and familiar regime. Revolutionary dictatorships like the Jacobins, Fascists and Communists achieved power by manipulating *populist* social movements but tended to grow *technocratic* with age. Before the regime becomes entrenched and stable, authoritarian revolutionaries may attempt to mobilize popular support and cater to some populist passions for revenge retribution and violence. Military coups imposed *authoritarian absolutist*

	Populist	Technocratic
Liberal Democracy	Democratically elected governments that function within limits set by liberal institutions to implement populist policies. For example, Greek governments, which accumulated foreign debt to finance party patronage before 2008.	The post-Second World War liberal democratic model. For example, the British and French states with their professional civil services.
Authoritarian Absolutism	Revolutionary dictatorships based on popular mobilization. Typically, in their early stages, for example, the Jacobins.	Bureaucratic dictatorships; for example, Napoleon's Empire and late-Communist bureaucratic socialism.
Liberal Authoritarianism	When liberal institutions are backed by the nobility or rising bourgeoisie, the monarch or dictator may adopt populist policies to ally with commoners against them; for example, in Wilhelmine Germany. Authoritarian liberal governments can generate populist protest from below; for example, in late Habsburg Austro-Hungary.	Authoritarian technocratic states limited by liberal independent institutions. For example, Habsburg Austro-Hungarian post-1848 state and contemporary Singapore.
Absolutist (Illiberal) Democracy	Populist democratically elected governments without liberal institutional constraints; for example, classic Greek and Roman democracies.	Democratically elected governments, unchecked by liberal institutions and led by technocrats; for example, the post-totalitarian democracies in Central Europe during 1990–2010.

technocracies to replace populist democracies numerous times in Latin America and most recently in Thailand and Egypt.

The *liberal* or Whig tradition traces its origins back to Magna Carta in the Middle Ages. It was theorized by Montesquieu, and put into practice by the founders of the United States in the eighteenth century. *Liberalism* was developed as a check on *absolutism*. Initially, this absolutism was monarchic. But liberal independent institutions limit and check any government, democratic, populist, or technocratic. Liberalism is particularly useful in checking the self-destructive aspects of populism. For example, the introduction of an independent Central Bank was an expansion of liberalism to check inflationary populist policies that democratic governments indulged in with abandon as late as the 1970s.

Liberal authoritarian governments are not elected and accountable. Political participation remains within prescribed local or sectoral bounds. Yet, the government is constrained by traditions and laws enforced by an independent judiciary. The press, religion, and civil society may be free and independent and check the power of the state. Liberal authoritarian regimes can be populist or technocratic, and are sometimes both, on different social and political levels: Since authoritarian rulers do not need to win elections, they can implement technocratic unpopular policies, for example fight populist racism and painfully restructure and modernize the economy. But since the subjects cannot affect policies and political parties cannot have real political power, they can express extreme populist political passions without having to worry about their potentially self-destructive effects.

Populist politics can express protest against authoritarian technocracy. Liberal authoritarianism can result in political bifurcation between powerful technocratic elite and populist powerless populace. For example, the

Austro-Hungarian Empire, at least since 1848, was liberal and authoritarian. The liberal elite respected the rule of law, protected minorities, and encouraged political and social integration in a multi-ethnic empire, economic modernization, and social mobility. At the same time, the disenfranchised multitude was free to harbor and express ethnic passions and rage without the risk of suffering political consequences, at least until the First World War and the rise of populist absolute democracies from the ashes of the empire, followed by populist absolute authoritarian regimes (with the exception of Czechoslovakia, which remained democratic, multi-national and quite liberal). Singapore is a contemporary technocratic liberal authoritarian state. Like Austro-Hungary it is a multi-ethnic society where a liberal technocratic elite suppresses both populism and democracy while respecting the rule of law (Rajah 2012). To different extents, Asian "tigers" like South Korea and Taiwan were also authoritarian liberal technocracies, though they had different degrees of liberalism and have moved by different degrees toward democracy. These countries became prosperous because they had competent technocratic elites that managed liberal institutions, not because they were authoritarian.

Democratic absolutism (in other words *illiberal democracy*) is the topic of this book. In the absence of robust liberal institutions, this is a 'winner takes all' democratic majoritarian political system, where the decisions of the majority or of a decisive significant minority are not balanced or checked by liberal institutions. A representative majority is not encumbered by tradition and law, and can suppress minorities unprotected by rights. The popular assembly or representative body can continuously change the law, case by case, to fit its momentary interests or passions. Absolute democracy can transition smoothly to authoritarianism in the absence of liberal institutions to slow or stop the slide. A temporary majority can change the rules of democratic elections to impose the perpetual rule of a minority. One of the reasons for majorities to respect minority rights is the prospect of becoming a minority in the future. If the majority expects to be permanent, it loses a reason for self-constraint. As Huey Long put it: "There is no dictatorship in Louisiana. There is a perfect democracy there, and when you have a perfect democracy it is pretty hard to tell it from a dictatorship" (quoted in Signer 2009, 120). The modern twist on this old, old, story is a new type of transition, from populist liberal democracy, gradually through illiberal democracy, to the old authoritarian destination.

Before the emergence of the *liberal-democratic* synthesis, all democracies were absolutist. Classical absolutist democracies had elaborate election systems, including random choice by lottery, and governing bodies to check the powers of *individuals*, but no liberal institutions to check the powers of majorities and of the *state*. Populist absolute democracy typically led through social conflict to authoritarianism. Liberalism developed in England to limit the powers of the monarchy. By the time democratization had progressed gradually in the long nineteenth century, the liberal institutions had already been entrenched and established in England and its former colonies for centuries. By contrast, the national democracies that succeeded the multi-national empires after the First World War had no such entrenched native liberal institutions, norms, and political habits. They had to try to establish liberalism and democracy at the same time, quickly. With the exception of Czechoslovakia and Finland, they failed at both.

Illiberal democracies can be technocratic or populist. Technocratic illiberal democracies can enact rationalizing reforms quickly without the constraints of checks, balances, and active civil society. The post-Communist transplanting of liberal democracy appeared deceptively easy because it encountered no resistance, but it had no liberal social foundations either. Totalitarianism handed over a political blank slate because it had eliminated all political power centers that could have resisted reforms.

Post-totalitarian states inherited the absence of rule of law, checks and balances, and an atomized, ineffective civil society (Tucker 2015). These illiberal properties facilitated radical, and painful economic restructuring, colloquially called "shock therapy." Unlike in populist democratic Southern Europe, post-Communist governments did not need to borrow to keep their atomized and passive civil society from unseating them. At the same time and for the same reasons, the post-Communist technocratic elite was able to enjoy high levels of personal corruption. In the post-Communist countries, democracy took root immediately, while liberal institutions and traditions evolved gradually for twenty years, after transplantation in a rough soil. Then, following the recession and the perception of corrupt and self-serving elites, technocratic democracy turned populist. This technocracy had already stronger liberal institutions than in 1989, but they were still weaker than in older liberal democracies. Progress toward liberalism was then halted, its growth stunted and, finally, in Hungary it was drawn and quartered in the prime of life.

India is another case of democratic transition to populist neo-illiberalism from a technocracy. India inherited at its founding technocratic liberal democratic institutions and bureaucracies that gained popularity as alternatives to populist decision making. Like the United States, India imported traditional liberal institutions that originated in Britain. But growing populism led to authoritarianism during Indira Gandhi's "National Emergency" rule (1975–1977). The liberal democratic restoration in the late 1970s strengthened some liberal institutions like the Supreme Court, but political populism persisted on the national level and managed to win elections on the local level. Indian technocracy gave way to populism, and populism pushed politics in a neo-illiberal direction to attack and overwhelm the liberal institutions, using some of the legal means that had been established during the authoritarian phase. India has retained its democracy along with some liberal aspects, like a vibrant civil society and legal profession. But the victories of the ruling BJP and prime minister Modi in elections in 2014 and 2019 led to a struggle between an increasingly neo-illiberal state and its liberal institutions, as the state expanded to take over educational and legal institutions, and replace technocrats with populists (Chatterji et al. 2019). The source of India's questionable policies is not democracy as Zakaria (2003) implied, but neo-illiberal populism. As in other neo-illiberal democracies, the process of transition from technocratic liberal democracy via populism to illiberalism in India has been gradual. The geographical size and demographic diversity and size of India, like that of the United States, are natural barriers to strong central governments, including neo-illiberal ones.

The Scope of Neo-Illiberal Democracy

This book is a political theory of contemporary, modern, and therefore *neo*-illiberal democracy. The scope is wide, including post-Communist countries in Central Europe, political movements and members of coalition governments in Western Europe, the Republican Party in the United States, Israel's Likud government, India's BJP government, and Brazil's Bolsonaro. The neo-illiberal focus excludes from the scope of the book illiberal or authoritarian states that have never been liberal such as Russia, the Philippines, and Turkey. Authoritarian regimes that attempted to use some veneers of liberal legality and democracy, but have never been liberal and were only selectively democratic when it suited their interests and the results could be guaranteed, like Russia, Turkey, the post-reconstruction confederate states, and so on, are beyond the scope of the book.

Russia was an imperialist late-totalitarian dictatorship that imploded. In the 1990s, the state became very weak and, consequently, an unregulated and unprotected space for freedom emerged spontaneously, for civil society such as it was, as well as for crime and corruption. But Russia has never had liberal institutions, not even state independent religion and property rights. Following Putin's restoration, the old secret police elite reasserted its control over a stronger though still quite weak state. Russian liberal-democracy did not die; it was stillborn.

In Turkey, a decades-long power struggle between a secular, modernizing, and authoritarian military and Islamist populists ended with the dramatic suppression of a military coup and the establishment of a hybrid authoritarian populist regime. During this struggle, the Islamists used democratic legitimacy against the military. But they never constructed liberal institutions, nor has there been much of a constituency for liberalism in Turkey outside the big cities of Istanbul and Ankara. The Turkish judiciary and press, though less weak than they are today, have never wielded the independent power they possess in liberal democracies. Erdogan's post-coup consolidation of power and suppression of political opponents mark the end of the institutional independence of the military, and its submission to the state. The military is not a liberal institution.

After the defeat of the Confederacy in the American Civil War, the occupying Unionists forced abolition and democracy until they stopped enforcing the second, which led to undemocratic (Democratic Party) single-party rule. Democracy was foreign to the South and so it did not die there, but ceased to be enforced from without.

The liberal institutions of illiberal states in Latin America, like Venezuela and Ecuador, have been too weak for those states to be considered neo-illiberal rather than absolutist-illiberal or authoritarian. Their political permutations took place within broader cycles of populist democracy and authoritarianism, neither of which has been liberal. The Latin American transitions from democracy to authoritarianism were too quick to have encountered resistance from viable liberal institutions; they displayed none of the back and forth pushing and shoving between the executive and liberal institutions that is so typical of neo-illiberal democracy, and creates much of the sound and fury that surrounds it. Authoritarian regimes ebb and flow for internal and external reasons. Without pre-existing liberal institutions, there can be no *neo*-illiberal democracy.

There are obvious similarities in the "tool kit of dirty tricks" that authoritarian and illiberal regimes, including neo-illiberal ones, use to muzzle the press, centralize control of the branches of government, and persecute their opponents. They have obviously imitated and learned from each other. However, conceptually *neo*-illiberal democracy must be a *liberal democracy* to some noticeable degree first. Only then can democratically elected governments seek to "de-liberalize" the state, by inventing, borrowing, or imitating, by design or coincidence, the methods of authoritarians who meet weaker or no resistance when they consolidate authoritarianism, transfer power from one authoritarian elite to another, or expand an already illiberal state to destroy resistance in institutions or civil society. The similarities between Turkey and Poland, the United States and Russia, are only in some "symptoms" but not in the underlying etiology.

The British Brexit political crisis was initiated by the top-down introduction of an illiberal democratic instrument, the plebiscite, which had never been part of the British liberal unwritten constitution, though it was used before a few times in a consultative form and once (over changing the electoral system in 2011) in a binding form. This illiberal populist measure led predictably if unintendedly to a populist result. Other populist themes like xenophobia emerged subsequently in British politics. However, none of this amounts to neo-illiberalism or even to an attempt at neo-illiberalism. Britain is not and is not likely to become a neo-illiberal democracy, though it is likely to experiment with populist politics. British neo-illiberalism would have had to involve the British prime minister sacking the director of MI5 or the Special Branch before attacking the Lord Chief

Justice over corruption investigations, while violating the independence of the BBC and transforming it into a propaganda arm of the ruling party, either by appointing party hacks to direct it, or by selling it to a friendly oligarch. An illiberal British PM would further appoint politically loyal judges, who would allow the imposition of a new written constitution and electoral rules to guarantee permanent gerrymandered majorities for the ruling party. The ruling party would also replace apolitical civil servants with party operatives and exercise direct control over the Bank of England. In England, last but not least, the government could instruct the Queen to dismiss the Archbishop of Canterbury and replace him with a politically loyal cleric, should he refuse to grant divine sanction to government policies. Sounds like an idea for a TV mini-series entitled "A Very Un-British Coup," or a movie plot for Rowan Atkinson? England then is not about to transmute into a neo-illiberal democracy, even if it may have populist democratic governments at least in ideology if not in practice.

This book does not analyze "left-wing populism" because it is not illiberal, and it is unclear whether it is even properly populist. The media calls radical left-wing parties like Syriza in Greece, Podemos in Spain, the Democratic Socialists who supported Senator Bernie Sanders, and so on "left-wing populists." Neo-illiberal governments, whether of the right or left, must have conflicts with liberal institutions such as the judiciary. For example, during the years 1935 to 1937, F. D. Roosevelt's executive came into such conflicts with the judiciary branch of government in the United States over the new deal's left-leaning reforms. The Supreme Court attempted to block the new deal and, in response, Roosevelt planned on packing the Supreme Court with political loyalists, which in effect would have curtailed its independence. That would have been an aspect of left-wing illiberalism.

But nothing of the sort happened during the four years (2015–2019) Syriza was in power. I have seen no evidence that any of the "left-wing populist" parties or groups between social democracy and the Trotskyite vanguard have any such intentions. While the Greek governments that preceded Syriza were definitely populist (though not necessarily left wing) because their policies led to the destruction of the Greek economy, Syriza's policies, aside from its ideology, were not populist. To avoid austerity, they did not want to pay back the loans of the Greek state. This was in the Greek national interest. It came into conflict with the interests of the European Union in general and Germany in particular. Since the latter held all the cards, they imposed their interests on the Greeks. This is not populist politics, but realist politics of interests. Maybe, if Syriza had not been so constrained, it would have embarked on economic populism that would have seriously hurt the Greek economy, but the fact of the matter is that it did not.

If populist left-wing rhetoric became policy, it may lead to a Venezuelan-type implosion through state over-spending beyond its means and credit. But it is far from clear that any of the so called "left-wing populist" parties would actually follow their own rhetoric. More significantly, it is unclear whether, if facing clear and immediate "Venezuelan" prospects, they would not step back from the brink, change course, and accept the constraints of the world we live in to become ordinary center-left governments. For example, when François Mitterrand's socialists came into power in a coalition with the Communist Party in 1981 France, they sang the *International* on the day of their victory and attempted to implement left-wing populist policies. Within two years, they had to correct their course to prevent a crisis turning into a catastrophe, and ruled for the rest of the 1980s successfully as conventional center-left social democrats. As governments have come to rely increasingly on refinancing their debts on the international markets, the first sign of distress is usually rising costs of borrowing, which makes it more difficult for governments to pay their bills. They must choose then between default (as the populists do) or anti-populist austerity and reform (as ordinary center-left politicians do). Politicians, including "left-wing populists," make promises that they cannot or do not intend to fulfil. The real test of populism is of policy.

The undoubtedly passionate aspect of left-wing politics is the fanatic insistence of left-wing populist voters on voting for a politician who expresses precisely their convictions, ideals, and passions. Populist left-wing voters shun compromises for the sake of building a broader, less ideologically purist, coalition that can actually stand a chance of achieving a democratic majority and face the test of cold reality. This is passionate political populism in its obvious self-destructiveness, guaranteeing fragmentation and political defeats.

Weimar, Jackson, Singapore

This book is a late addition to the burgeoning "political apocalypse now" genre of books about the death of democracy, the twilight of civilization, and the return of ideological mortality to history. It benefits from this late coming. This is not a knee jerk or hysterical reaction to a shock, nor a desperate cry for help, nor the thought of somebody who was pushed off a skyscraper and tells himself half way down "so far so good." The theoretical analysis I propose in this book offers a historically and comparatively founded theoretical alternative to a few earlier popular interpretations of the politics of the second decade of the twenty-first century, which I call *Weimarian,* *Jacksonian,* and *Singaporean*:

Weimarian interpretations perceived a global acidic wave of authoritarianism, corroding and washing away the achievements of the postwar reconstruction in Western Europe, the Civil Rights Movement in the United States, and the "third wave" of democratization in Southern

Europe, Latin America, and East Europe. An apparently similar "tidal wave" in the 1920s and 1930s undid the achievements of the post-First-World-War Wilsonian world order of self-determining liberal-democratic nation-states in a peaceful community of nations. The current "wave," like its predecessor almost a century earlier, does not have a single common source or explanation. It resembles an unconditional *zeitgeist*, a historical trend that spreads partly by imitation and partly for unknown common or separate reasons, like colonialism or nationalism. *Weimarians* tend to conflate authoritarianism, illiberalism, and populism and, taken to extremes, reduce them all to "Adolf." If this analysis is correct, the liberal institutional defenses are so weak that a chance occurrence, such as a terrorist attack like the one that burnt the Reichstag in 1933, or the 9/11 attacks on New York and Washington, may provide the excuse to bring down the democratic house of cards and establish illiberal authoritarianism. It may be that by pure luck there has been no such destabilizing terrorist attack and liberals let their guards down, until Covid-19 reshuffled the political cards and took all political bets off.

If this process is beyond anybody's control, we might as well try to enjoy cabarets, while waiting for the gestapo. This interpretation emerged following the surprising rolling shocks of the successes of Trump's rhetoric, Trump's victory in the republican primaries and, above all, his victory in the 2016 elections. People who experienced or were directly affected by the Second World War (Albright 2018), or historians specializing in the study of that period (Snyder 2017), were particularly receptive to this kind of interpretation, though other historians who studied Nazism (Herf 2016a, 2016b) acknowledged some of the similarities, but also emphasized the differences. As Runciman (2018, 31) put it, Europeans and North Americans are too prosperous, old, networked, and with knowledge of history to repeat the end of Weimar. "Political violence is a young man's game." Too much of the 1930s is missing: current illiberal democracies have no militias and no unemployed risk loving and not just taking military veterans to man them. Most European countries have experienced demographic declines, especially in post-Communist countries where mass emigration combined with low fertility. Wealthier societies and welfare states have lower levels of misery in severe recessions than poorer and less secure workers did during the 1930s. Populist leaders this time depend on weak and fickle popular support that is not sufficient for starting costly wars, unless they can be won quickly and decisively. The liberal institutions in some countries with neo-illiberal governments or movements are more resistant and resilient than those of the Weimar Republic. As Levitsky and Ziblatt (2018) emphasized, globally the number of democratic backslides is balanced by democracies that stabilized. The total number of democracies in the world has not changed much since 2005. Thomas Carothers, who attacked the transition-to-democracy "paradigm," co-authored an article in *Foreign Affairs* entitled "Democracy is not Dying: Seeing through the Doom and Gloom." There may be an illiberal wave, but it is far from a tsunami, and there are other waves pushing the ships of state in opposite directions.

History, however, rhymes rather than repeats itself. The final dramatic push toward authoritarianism from neo-illiberal democracy, "the burning Reichstag," kind of event some analysts were expecting, as I write now in April of 2020, may not be terrorism, as many had worried, but the return of a pandemic plague after a hundred years – the spread of the coronavirus. The kinds of authoritarian measures that may be necessary to contain the spread of the disease are conducive to a permanent state of emergency and a permanent slide from neo-illiberal democracy to authoritarianism. A telling sign is that Hungary's Orbán entirely abolished the constitutional power of the parliament that his Fidesz Party controlled anyway. In March of 2020, the Hungarian parliament

passed a law that rhymed with the German Enabling
Act of March 1933, which gave Hitler the right to rule
by decree, following the burning of the Reichstag and a
disinformation campaign about an impending Communist
coup. The Hungarian parliament suspended its own
constitutional powers and transferred to the government
the right to rule by decree and prosecute those who
"distribute misinformation." The difference is that the
Nazis did not have a parliamentary majority and so they
had to arrest their opponents in order to have a majority,
whereas Orbán the illiberal democrat already had a parliamentary majority that was ready to make itself politically
powerless. Orbán's use of an apparent emergency as a
pretext is as obvious as it had been during the refugee
crisis. As much as Hungary had one of the lowest rates in
the EU of refugees trying to settle there, it also had one of
the lowest mortality rates from the coronavirus in Europe,
less than a percentage of that of Italy when the law passed.
Obviously, suspension of civil rights and the powers of
the parliament will not save a single soul. The worst-hit
European countries at that stage, Italy and Spain, did not
take any steps away from liberal democracy in response to
the crisis, let alone suspend parliament.

Meanwhile, in Israel Netanyahu used the crisis and the
health restrictions on public gathering in Israel to suspend
the courts that should have tried him for corruption and
to suspend the activity of the parliament where, following
the elections, his coalition parties had a narrow minority.
Israel's Supreme Court ruled against the government
and in favor of the parliament. But then Netanyahu
was successful in following the neo-illiberal tried-and-
tested book of tricks, where it is not necessary to have
a majority, as long as the majority is sufficiently divided
against itself. As I write in April, he may well neutralize
the courts by controlling the appointments of new judges
and have a new "emergency" government that would not
undo the damage his government has already inflicted on
Israel's liberal institutions, if not expand it.

Historically, societies have committed plenty of irrational hysterical actions, including sliding to political fanaticism or authoritarianism during plagues. Athens lost the Peloponnesian War, followed by the rule of the thirty tyrants, following a plague. Desperate Florentines turned to Savonarola's fanatical theocratic authoritarianism at the height of another plague. No doubt neo-illiberals are watching the results of the dramas in Hungary and Israel and making plans for their own countries. A continuous state of medical emergency and a spreading plague are good covers for suspending or stealing elections. Still, historical experiences demonstrate that the political results of plagues more often than not tend to be temporary and disappear with them. After plagues, surviving Europeans preferred to forget and try to resume their lives where they left them. Older European cities are marked by plague columns constructed to mark the end of plagues and the restoration of the older order. We may be building political as well as epidemiological columns before long. After the plagues, politics tends to return to the status quo ante, though there are longer-term economic and social changes. The big unknown as I write is how long it will take scientists to bring this plague under control, find cures, a vaccine, and then vaccinate the population, to bring this historical episode of the plague to an end. Hungary and Israel were neo-illiberal democracies before the plague and the results of the struggle between the executive and legislative and judiciary branches of government following the plague reflect how far neo-illiberal democracy had already proceeded down the road in each country; all the authoritarian way in Hungary, and half way in Israel. So far, in this early stage, in countries that had not been on the road to illiberalism and authoritarianism already before the plague, the plague increased the popularity of incumbents irrespective of their politics, but had few other apparent political effects.

Indian neo-illiberalism has been violent and involved militias of young men. Yet, it does not falsify Runciman's thesis above because India is not as prosperous or old as the first-world countries who turned to neo-illiberalism. Though Hindu illiberalism turned into violence against Moslem Indians, that violence was not distinctly neo-illiberal or a new political phenomenon in India. Intercommunal and political violence in India has preceded illiberalism. Violence has been a feature of Indian majoritarian politics. The new neo-illiberal element is the retreat of the federal state from its secular liberalism that should have protected minorities from the state, though not from their neighbors.

The opposite *Jacksonian* interpretation gained credibility when the Reichstag failed to ignite, the storm troopers made it as far as Charlottesville Virginia, but failed to arrive in the cities, and life seemed to go on for many people who were not refugees, immigrants, or members of minorities but remained in their intact social and economic bubbles; though, as I write, the plague hits the cities and the social and economic bubbles are being punctured. Previously, some people were able to tell themselves that over the centuries, democracy resulted in many types of governments, some quite unsavory. Arguably, today's neo-illiberal populism is unexceptional in comparison with previous populist episodes such as the presidency of Andrew Jackson, an uncouth representative of rural frontier America, who supported slavery and resented the urban, educated, wealthy parts of the country. Democracy in America and its liberal independent institutions survived Jackson. Donald Trump himself seems to encourage such an interpretation. He hung a portrait of Jackson in the Oval Office and paid a respectful visit to Jackson's gravesite, though some of his statements indicated that he was not too familiar with the history of Jackson's presidency and when he lived. Arguably, populism ebbs and flows, while democracy and liberal institutions persist. All democracies have some populist aspects. As long as populism does not dominate government policies, the system can contain it without becoming self-destructive. People do not die each time they indulge in an excessive piece of cake or smoke a cigar. At least not immediately.

Yet, though the current crisis has been fueled by populism, and the dramatic noises of populism drown the steady droning of neo-illiberalism, its substance is neo-*illiberal* democracy, the unprecedented systematic attempt to deconstruct the independent branches and institutions of the liberal state. Populist president Jackson was a lawyer and he knew better than to challenge the constitution, such as it was, allowing slavery. The most extreme challenge president Jackson posed to liberal institutions was in his struggle with the Bank of the United States (Signer 2009). A comparable contemporary liberal populist to Jackson is Trump's first Attorney General, former Alabama senator Jeff Sessions, a populist xenophobe and likely racist, but also a liberal in respecting the constitution and the separation of powers. Trump, Orbán, Kaczyński, and so on, by contrast, are strictly illiberal. They have no respect for the rule of law and the institutions in charge of enforcing it.

The final *Singaporean* misinterpretation of neo-illiberal democracy is Hungary's prime minister Viktor Orbán's deliberate misrepresentation of illiberal democracy as resembling Singapore's government. Orbán attempted to confuse a prosperous technocratic liberal authoritarianism with its diametrical opposite, populist neo-illiberal democracy. Using the dialectical trope of totalitarian rhetoric, the identification between opposites, Orbán attempted to associate his regime with the successful modernization and wealth of its political opposite. Singapore enjoys the rule of law and independent judiciary and government free of corruption, though with authoritarian limitations on political freedoms and the freedom of the press (Rajah 2012). It is rich and attracts immigrants. Hungary is the opposite. It is among the five poorest members of the European Union on a per capita basis, and its skilled and young workers try to move to more liberal countries.

Plan of the Book

The strategic plan of the book is to move from a general historically based comparative study of illiberal democracy to the current crisis of populist neo-illiberal democracy, its causes and scenarios for its future. The current predicament raises general questions about its historical evitability. Finally, on the basis of the previous chapters, I propose policy reforms that may preempt similar recurrences in the future, laying the foundations for new liberalism without nostalgia.

The next chapter, "Old Hemlock in Plastic Cups," examines what neo-illiberal democracy is by comparing ancient and modern forms of absolutist democracy.

The third chapter, "All the Roads Lead to Caesarea," examines the two types of path dependencies that have led to neo-illiberal democracy recently: Post-totalitarian technocratic to populist illiberalism, as it developed in Hungary and Poland; and the post-liberal populist illiberalism of established liberal democracies like the United States and Israel. I argue that neo-illiberal democracies are inherently unstable. They may result in a Caesarian transition to stable authoritarianism, or in a stable liberal restoration. Other scenarios are less probable.

The fourth chapter, "It Ain't Necessarily So: The Historical Evitability of Neo-Illiberal Democracy," examines the causes of neo-illiberalism. It argues for two mutually reinforcing large linear causes, atavistic misinterpretation of economic crises as evolutionary extinction events, and the blocking of social mobility. Numerous additional small non-linear causes were necessary for the apparent wave of populist neo-illiberal democracy. Therefore, this wave was evitable. It could have easily been otherwise and it may be reversed for similarly minute and non-linear causes.

The final chapter, "New Liberalism without Nostalgia," proposes policy prescriptions. It is divided into three parts: first I propose measures for the preemption of populism; then, I suggest how to remove barriers to social mobility; finally, I suggest measures to strengthen liberal institutions. My policy recommendations are mostly "blue sky" or "loonshots," and decidedly *non-nostalgic*. Unlike many political programs, I do not advocate a return to any "golden age." I do not think the past was as great as nostalgia paints it, and I do not think it can be restored. Instead, I advocate the opposite of neo-illiberal democracy, new-liberal democracy. I outline what new liberalism may mean for the contemporary irreversibly globalized world, marked by syncretism more than universalism.

2

Illiberal Democracy: Old Hemlock in Plastic Cups

Democracy had had a reputation for being historically short, aggressively nasty, and politically brutish, until the late nineteenth century. The democratic elements in the American Revolution were presented as "republican" (Sartori 1987). Educated people associated democracy with populist absolutism, the rule of mobs motivated by fickle self-consuming political passions, or concretely, with the rules of the demagogues in Athens. After the civil strife and violence of democracy, peaceful and stable Hellenic or Roman authoritarianism came as a relief. After a century of republican democratic civil strife, Roman authoritarianism lasted for half a millennium, or a millennium and a half if the Eastern Roman Empire counts. During those imperial centuries, the empire adopted a new universal religion, became multi-ethnic and multicultural, expanded and contracted, extended citizenship to all, went through countless palace coups and political upheavals, yet not even once was there a serious attempt or even an argument for an attempt to restore democracy or the republic.

De Maistre in his *Study on Sovereignty* ridiculed democracy as inherently populist and self-destructive. "To hear ... defenders of democracy talk, one would think that the people deliberate like a committee of wise men, whereas in truth judicial murders, foolhardy undertakings, wild choices, and above all foolish and disastrous wars are eminently the prerogatives of this form of government." When de Maistre was writing, he had good historical reasons for his opinions, following the fates of democracies in Greece and Rome. The French Revolution that inspired him seemed to repeat the terror and wars of the late Roman Republic. A quick overview of this history of absolutist democracy is useful for putting contemporary neo-illiberal democracy in its proper historical comparative context.

The Self-Destruction of Absolute Democracy

Ancient democracies excluded most residents, slaves, aliens, and women. They were "impoverished, slave-holding, militaristic oligarchies, which managed to consume themselves in class warfare" (Holmes 1995, 32). Though neo-illiberal democracies are more inclusive, they share a tendency toward populist self-destruction. Oddly, while there were quick "reductions to Adolf" in the press and the democratic apocalypse scholarly literature, there have been hardly any mentions of Cleon and Cleophon of Athens or of the century of civil wars and revolutions in Rome that led to the establishment of the empire and its acquiescing acceptance by exhausted demographically decimated Roman republicans.

Ancient democracy and its populist self-destruction had been at the background and projected foreground of all debates about democracy and constitutionalism until an unprecedented modern regime, totalitarianism, consigned classical tyrannies and democracies to irrelevant oblivion. The ancient demagogues and tyrants could not explain the originality of Stalin or Hitler in power. Modi, Trump, Netanyahu, and Orbán, by contrast, would have felt at home and looked familiar to the average fourth-century-BCE Athenian. The similar patterns are inescapable:

Cleon the Athenian demagogue gained power when Athens could not win a long war led by aristocratic experts, despite significant Athenian sacrifices. Unlike previous Athenian leaders, Cleon was a successful businessman with no familial political legacy, before he was democratically elected a general (the Athenians elected their military commanders). He used his inarticulate speech, full of expletives, gestures, and shouts, ignorance, and contempt for high culture, to gain street credibility with the lower classes. Cleon encouraged the use of private lawsuits for treason to persecute and intimidate his political enemies, in the absence of liberal defenses of individual rights. This strategy killed Socrates. Cleon called for self-interested, amoral, and brutally realistic foreign policy. He manipulated passions to trump civic virtues. The result was risky military aggression that led to the destruction of Athens from without, and civil war from within.

Under demagogues like Cleon, Athenians voted on the results of trials irrespective of traditional law and precedence. For example, following the battle of Arginusae in 406 BCE the Athenian Assembly tried and condemned to death eight generals and executed six, including the son of Pericles. The generals won the battle, but at great losses, due to stormy weather that prevented salvaging sailors who fell off board. Xenophon wrote that some in the Assembly argued that the proceeding went against the law, but others retorted that the people rather than traditional law had the ultimate authority. To compound the folly, the assembly rejected a peace offer from Sparta, which led to Athens' defeat in the Peloponnesian War in 405 (Thucydides 2009; Mitchell 2015). Samons recites the litany of self-destructive Athenian populist democratic absolutist policies and decisions: To make war on their former friends and allies, to execute their leaders, to extort payments from allied states that wished to be free of Athenian hegemony and use the proceeds for more extortions, to execute and enslave thousands of other Greeks, to start wars of aggression that could not have been cost effective, to refuse to help allies in war, and so on. He balanced those decisions against better decisions, for example during the Persian Wars, to conclude that: "it would ... be difficult to construct a list of praiseworthy or wise Athenian votes in the classical period that could rival in number those ballots that to many moderns (and at least some ancient Greeks) have seemed unjust, belligerent, or simply foolish." (Samons 2004, 51)

The democratic restoration in Athens in 403 BCE after the overthrow of an oligarchy restored a mild version of the rule of law that recognized the primacy of traditional law to decrees and the will of any assembly. But the judiciary was not professional or independent; the composition of the courts was decided by lottery, and there was no constitution to constrain assemblies and jurors.

Plato and Aristotle characterized the demagogues and, by extension, democracy, as appealing to the baser emotions, passions and prejudices, rather than to reason. Some more pro-democratic modern commentators like Moses Finlay distinguished demagogues who fit the platonic mold from ones who merely made promises that could not be fulfilled, which, with a great deal of anachronism, may be called left-wing populists. I want to emphasize against the ancients and some of the moderns that the Athenian oligarchs, including some of Socrates' students, were no models of platonic dispassionate aristocratic rational decision making. Hot-blooded young male members of the elite led by Alcibiades made their share of populist imperialist military blunders. The association of passionate populism *exclusively* with the lower classes follows ancient oligarchic anti-democratic propaganda. The weakness of all the ancient forms of government, democracy, oligarchy, or tyranny was that they were absolutist-illiberal. The passions of oligarchs may have been different from those of the lower classes, but either way, they ruled in a way that was dangerously unconstrained.

The self-destruction of the Roman Republic took over a century and proceeded through a historical procession of

demagogues who appealed especially to the large impoverished population of the city of Rome, composed largely
of veterans and impoverished farmers. The demagogues
themselves were members of the Roman elite, from the
Gracchi brothers to Julius Caesar, skilled in the fine arts of
mob manipulation, control of legions, and self-enrichment.
The proletarians, whose only property was their children,
were desperate for food and passionate for reality shows
in the arenas to satisfy their baser passions for blood and
gore. This extremely unequal social structure, constantly
augmented by more veterans, slaves, extorted taxes, and
wheat from the wars and the empire, would destabilize
any regime, whether absolute or liberal. But the root cause
of the crisis was what I call *elite populism*: The republican
elite, the senatorial class, succumbed to its passions, to
avarice, to pay for what they recognized as luxury. The
republican elite was nostalgic for simpler times when the
republic was based on republican citizen-farmers. But
nostalgia did not stop them from enriching themselves
from the empire in ways that made farming uneconomic.
The farmers could not compete with free grains raised as
tributes and taxes. The populism of the republican elite
caused then the populism of the impoverished urban lower
classes and the eventual destruction of the republic and
the republican elite itself. The elite that benefitted from
the empire could not bring itself to institute the kind of
reforms that would have eliminated this destabilizing
proletariat, such as retreat from the empire, emancipation
of the slaves and gladiators, and a return to a republican
order founded on citizen-farmers who, when needed,
were also soldiers. This republican ideal was the origin of
Jeffersonian republicanism.

Jumping across two undemocratic millennia, the first
universal free and fair elections in human history, still
limited by gender to males but, for the first time, not
limited to a class by property prerequisites, or to members
of particular ethnic groups, took place in France in
1848. The result was the election of Louis Napoleon as

president of the Second Republic. Within half a year he abolished democracy and the freedom of the press. Within two years, he declared himself Emperor Napoleon. Louis Napoleon was elected nineteen centuries after the end of ancient republicanism in a populous industrial modern society yet, as a scion of a known family and a demagogue who appealed to the passions of his voters, he could have felt at home in the late Roman republic. The reason for the fast and facile transition from democracy to authoritarianism in France was the absence of liberal institutions and enough liberal-democrats to defend them. The French, given the opportunity to vote for the first time in history, selected the most personally ridiculous and dangerously anti- democratic candidate, whose charisma emanated from that of his tyrannical step uncle, Napoleon 1st, who ruined the democratic aspirations of the French Revolution and enveloped France in two decades of destructive wars that led to its defeat. Napoleon 3rd was a bit of a joke: as Karl Marx put it, when history repeats itself, it is first a tragedy and then a farce. From the vantage point of 2020 I may add that, for the third time, history repeats itself as a reality show.

Marx in his *18th Brumaire of Louis Napoleon* struggled to explain why universal franchise led to this result rather than to socialism, and fell back on the Jacobin explanation of democratic politics that go wrong, the people do not understand their own best common interest; they are manipulated by the elites. He also did not like the small farmers who voted for Louis Napoleon. Thomas Jefferson would have also been embarrassed by these results as the small farmers who voted for Louis Napoleon should have been the kind of virtuous citizen-republicans who serve as building blocks for the grand edifices of republics. The French farmers, unlike Jefferson, did not even own slaves. These results of the first universal male suffrage led the liberal Mill and Tocqueville to have second thoughts about extending the franchise to the poor (Holmes 1995, 32). Interestingly, Jon Elster (2018) argued for the evitability of the self-destruction of French democracy in the 1848 elections. Small regulatory changes in the French electoral system could have prevented the election of Louis Napoleon constitutionally. Later, I return to the contingency and evitability of neo-illiberal democracy.

Jumping another century, to the end of the First World War; it led to the construction of what Ian Kershaw (2015) called "facade-democracies," without functioning liberal institutions and liberal-democratic majorities. The majorities did not respect the rights of minorities, and the minorities did not accept the verdicts of the majorities. The new nations that succeeded the empires after the First World War retained the populist aggressions that plunged them into that catastrophically self-destructive war, only with greater popular legitimacy because after the war the franchise was extended to lower classes, including peasants and workers, who pushed politics further to populist extremes. The war brutalized a generation of young people from peasant and working backgrounds and then gave them the right to vote in countries that had previously limited the franchise by wealth and class. These new democracies were divided between illiberal hard left and right, large land owners, and impoverished peasants longing for agrarian reforms, urban middle classes and workers and rural interests. States that were parts of the Russian and Ottoman sphere had no liberal traditions or institutions. States that emerged from the Habsburg Empire had some liberal institutions and technocratic bureaucracies skilled at operating them. But the populist passions associated with ethno-nationalism, and self–destructive economic policies led to the populist self-destruction of all the post-imperial democracies, except for Finland and Czechoslovakia. Most of this self-destruction took place prior to the rolling economic shocks and social crises of the post-1929 depression that led to the more famous Nazi takeover of Germany. Liberal institutions, prosperity and modernization probably account in whole or in part for the Finnish and Czechoslovak successes, as well as the coincidental, or not, fact that both Finnish and Czechoslovak state founders and leaders of national movement were professional philosophers, a fact that Plato would have celebrated, had he been a democrat, which of course he was not.

The planting of fragile democracies in harsh illiberal soils at the Paris Peace Conference in 1919 was influenced by US President Woodrow Wilson's policy of promoting national self-determination and democracy even in the absence of liberal institutions, traditions, independent and self-reliant Jeffersonian democrats, and in radically divided societies. The same Wilsonian ideals would live again a hundred years later, in the ideals of the American interventions to promote democracy in countries entirely innocent of liberalism like Iraq and Libya, predictably with similar success.

Since the Second World War, this sorry history of self-destructive absolute-illiberal democracies and its memory have been surpassed and suppressed. In the contexts of the struggle between liberal-democracies and the totalitarian Nazi and Communist regimes, the distinction between democracy and liberalism was overlooked and forgotten. Fears of the destructive passions of mobs were replaced with declarations of faith in the wisdom of the common people. In his speech to the American Congress when the United States joined the Second World War, Churchill celebrated faith in the common man as part of the shared democratic values of the two allies.

The repressed history of illiberal democracy has returned in the second decade of the twenty-first century with a vengeance. The question is: How and why did classical absolutist-illiberal democracy, warts and all, make a comeback after nearly a century of dormancy? History does not repeat itself, though it rhymes. So, the comparison with classical illiberal democracy should clarify what has changed and how neo-illiberal democracy differs from its classical versions.

Neo-Illiberal Unbalancing of the Liberal Checks

Neo-illiberal democracy is distinct from its classical absolutist predecessor in its war of attrition against liberal institutions, to uncheck and unbalance the state. Neo-illiberal democracy attempts to gradually bring about the *evisceration*, or *deconsolidation* if not *deconstruction* of liberal institutions. Ancient absolute democracies had no liberal institutional checks and balances to fight against. The "drama" of neo-illiberal democracy consists of permanent war between the democratically elected illiberal executive and the liberal institutions designed to curb its powers, the judiciary, law enforcement agencies, the Central Bank, independent mass media, civic society, and non-governmental organizations.

Neo-illiberal democratic governments are weak in comparison with totalitarian and authoritarian governments. They do not use the secret police to kill, imprison, terrorize, fragment, and manipulate the population. The military remains apolitical; neo-illiberal governments cannot use it to settle domestic disputes. Neo-illiberal governments cannot rely on the support of minorities whose rights they do not respect or on the alienated and resentful half of the population that does not vote for them. Emotional manipulation of self-destructive passions is naturally fickle and difficult to maintain. Therefore, to have absolute power, neo-illiberal governments must weaken countervailing liberal institutions, checks, and balances.

Democratically elected neo-illiberal governments conduct a war of attrition, not a blitz. The battle line with the liberal institutions may move to and fro and defensive lines on either side may hold for a while. There is no one single turning point; no declaration of emergency and suspension of democracy and its institutions; no surrounding of the presidential palace with tanks. Since the changes are piecemeal, each one may seem small, innocuous, and insignificant. Their meaning becomes obvious when put together.

The spread of the coronavirus may eventually prove to be such an inflection point, at least for Hungary. But authoritarians and illiberals are not more effective in controlling the forces of nature than democrats. Populist voters are also quick to become disappointed, if not disillusioned, unless the illiberals and authoritarians get lucky and nature coincidentally or science intentionally turns to be on their side.

Ruling neo-illiberal democratic parties do not eliminate political opposition, as authoritarian and totalitarian regimes do. Rather, they weaken, harass, or bribe them. To create an uneven playing field they change electoral rules, gerrymander, use election commissions to disadvantage their opponents, and use bureaucratic means (=cheat) to make sure they win elections. American gerrymandering similarly limits voting in African American areas, while facilitating the voting of whites in the South by the density and location of voting booths, forcing African Americans to travel far and wait in long line to vote, or give up.

Hungary went further by granting postal ballot rights to two million ethnic Hungarians constituting 20 percent of the electorate, who live in neighboring countries and are presumably more nationalistic if they vote in elections to a neighboring country, while denying the many Hungarian emigres living elsewhere such absentee ballots. They are deterred from voting by having to travel to, and queue outside Hungarian consulates. Hungary offers the most mature case of neo-illiberal transition (Magyar 2016; Ginsburg and Huq 2018, 90–119; *Economist* 2019), so it is useful as an ideal model of mature neo-illiberal democracy.

The Judiciary

The rule of law, enforced by the judiciary, police, prosecutors, ombudsmen, general comptrollers, and numerous other officials, limits the powers of governments. For example, it should protect civil and human rights and should not allow ad hoc policies against minorities or political enemies. Neutralizing the judiciary can be achieved by packing the courts and prosecutor's office with politically loyal judges and prosecutors. Lowering the compulsory retirement age rids the system of older judges and prosecutors. The process of selecting new judges can then be controlled by the illiberal majority in the parliament. It is also possible to construct new judicial branches staffed exclusively by political loyalists to regulate areas of particular interest to the illiberal government. For example (Ginsburg and Huq 2018, 90–119), in Poland, the president refused to swear in the constitutional court judges voted in by the outgoing Civic Platform government. The new Law and Justice (PiS) dominated parliament, then changed the law governing the appointment of judges. The government increased the judicial quorum required for valid decisions to preempt anti-government judicial majorities and forced the constitutional court to hear cases in the order of their filing, to delay their decision about the newest legislation about the constitutional court until the new appointed judges were seated. This was followed by a standoff until a sufficient number of judges were replaced to give the government the majorities it needed. Within two years the Polish constitutional court was in illiberal government hands. In 2020, the government proceeded to enact the mass retirement of judges, allowed the justice minister to appoint senior judges who assign cases to judges, thereby controlling which politically sensitive cases would be adjudicated by which politically reliable judges and, above all, allowed the parliament to set a disciplinary chamber above the Supreme Court, appointed by the neo-illiberal president, to suspend and punish judges who stray from their instructions, thereby abolishing the independence of the judiciary. This neutralized the judiciary as a check on government legislation and actions.

Hungary's neo-illiberal government annulled all constitutional court decisions prior to 2011 and lowered the retirement age for judges. Hungarian prosecutor office, state audit office, ombudsman, statistical office and the constitutional court were used both to shield prime minister Orbán and his party, Fidesz's, corruption and to harass the opposition. In Israel, the neo-illiberal democratic coalition began a war of attrition to weaken the strong and entrenched judiciary. Each member of the coalition had its own set of grievances: The prime minister, Netanyahu, wanted to be protected from judicial review legislation to give him immunity against prosecution for corruption. Illiberal populist right-wing legislators wanted to neutralize the Supreme Court's protections of limited sets of human rights for ethnic minorities, Palestinians and Israeli Arabs. Orthodox religious parties wanted to protect their sectoral privileges against judicial review that could annul them on the basis of equality before the law. The government attempted to legislate exemptions from judicial review to certain laws on the neo-illiberal basis of the supremacy of the parliament to the judiciary. It also proceeded to appoint neo-illiberal sympathetic judges, when older judges reached retirement. The government was successful in appointing a politically loyal Ombudsman who has been self-limiting his authorities to the lower rungs of the bureaucracy, but it failed to protect the prime minister from prosecution, most notably for attempting illicitly to gain political control of the most influential Israeli daily newspaper. The coronavirus crisis allowed the government to suspend trials, including that of the prime minister. In negotiations over the construction of an emergency government to handle the crisis, the Likud Party demanded to influence the selection of new judges, and consequently the independence of the judiciary.

Illiberals need not have *total* control of the judiciary; they are not totalitarian. They do not care for the fate of most murderers, rapists, and pickpockets, nor do they care for the outcomes of most civil disputes between neighbors, divorcing couples, and business partners. These cases can be adjudicated by independent judges. It is sufficient for the neo-illiberals to guarantee that cases that are of interest to them: constitutional cases that affirm the neo-illiberal deconstruction or evisceration of liberal institutions; cases that affect the distribution of political power such as decisions on media ownership; and criminal cases that involve their personal corruption; are held by the prosecutor's office indefinitely, or are brought before judges who owe their loyalty to the neo-illiberals. Generally, the judiciary should serve and legitimize the absolutist power of the executive, by all means, from grand-theorizing about absolutist executive privileges down to excluding a popular candidate from elections by claiming that a form was wrongly filled in.

In the United States, Trump's neo-illiberals were unable to generate vacancies in the judiciary. Like his liberal predecessors and Israel's neo-illiberals, Trump's effect on the personnel composition of the judiciary depends on deaths and retirements, and hence is slow and gradual. Trump's efforts to eviscerate the rule of law were met by resistance from the populist but liberal Attorney General Sessions and the Justice Department, who defended the rule of law and the independence of the judiciary. Trump's next appointee, William Barr, is indeed an illiberal in theory and practice, who acts to promote and defend an absolutist presidency. However, it is telling that when Trump moved to legally frame his apparently most competitive political opponent at the time, Democrat Joe Biden, a classical neo-illiberal move, he could not use his own Justice Department and the American judiciary, but had to try to pressure the government of a young democracy with very weak liberal institutions to do his bidding. The American institutions were still too liberal for the task. Orbán, let alone Putin, would have suffered no such constraints.

Civil Service

Government bureaucracies are conservative, resistant to change, and used to following regulations and practices, liberal or illiberal, depending on their traditions. In post-totalitarian states the traditions are illiberal (Tucker 2015). In post-liberal states, the bureaucracy defends its liberal independence and political impartiality. Neo-illiberals in power may have to fight, then, against the autonomy of the bureaucracy, its impartial and universal rule following norms, and its political neutrality, to personalize its decisions and submit them to political hierarchy against political and personal enemies.

The conflict becomes manifest when civil servants fail to implement neo-illiberal instructions because they violate laws, regulations, or traditions. Attacks on the bureaucracy, or "deep state" as it is known among its populist enemies, are therefore common. The civil service can appeal to the judiciary as long as it is still independent, leak embarrassing details about illegal actions to the press, as long as sufficient parts of it are not controlled directly or indirectly by the illiberal government, and refuse to carry out instructions by challenging authority, or by inactivity.

Neo-illiberals fight to replace and discipline the bureaucracy. For example, the republican obsession with exposing the identity of the "whistleblower" who divulged president Trump's attempt to extort Ukraine to frame his political rival, the removal and firing of the witnesses who testified truthfully in Trump's impeachment trial *and their relatives*, and the earlier firing of Comey as head of the FBI, were all neo-illiberal attempts to gain control of the bureaucracy by personnel replacement and intimidation. If successful, the bureaucracy becomes an active part in a patronage network that facilitates corruption in the absence of the rule of law. Neo-illiberals then can use government contracts and appointments to favor businesses with links to the neo-illiberal leaders, or the leaders themselves. They may use state subsidies and grants to favor loyalists. Selective use of tax authorities may punish rivals and reward allies. These are not distinctive characteristics of neo-illiberal democracy, but neo-illiberal democracy must succeed a liberal democracy, so it must fight to corrupt the civil service.

Civil Society and Independent Institutions

Unlike totalitarian states, and like authoritarian governments, neo-illiberals do not attempt to abolish civil society. They are interested exclusively in independent organizations that are political or may be of assistance to their political enemies (they have no rivals, only enemies). Since neo-illiberal democrats do not recognize minority rights they oppose associations of minorities, or those for the protections of minority rights. They consider interest groups (NGOs, environmental groups, local groups with local interests, think tanks, even universities in the case of Hungary) fully political. Neo-illiberals are committed to destroying their enemies, rather than tolerating their rivals. They attempt to block their sources of finance by prohibiting foreign donations, expelling foreign donors, taxing donations, forcing the publication of the identities of donors, and then punishing donors by blocking them from state contracts and using the state to harass them. All these methods were used to different degrees in all the neo-illiberal states, and even to a small degree in the still liberal United States in the Trump administration's apparent exclusion of Amazon's cloud services from contracts with the pentagon.

Liberal states have many institutions that are independent of the state, though they are supported by public funds. The judiciary and religion (except in the United States and France) are the most ancient. Education, the media, and the Central Bank were added later. There are many more, from local tourist boards to government advisory committees. None of these liberal institutions existed in ancient absolutist democracies, where every office holder was voted for or selected randomly. Neo-illiberal democracy attempts to abolish some of that independence and submit these bodies to the central neo-illiberal government.

Self-serving bureaucracies in liberal states may misuse their independence and not serve the purposes for which their institutions were founded. Institutions such as state schools and universities, public services, state-run media, and so on, may require radical reforms to overcome resistance to change, inefficiency, and even corruption. When illiberals abolish their independence, they cite these reasons, and they are not always wrong. But their reforms are illiberal because they rarely address these problems. Instead they are only interested in submitting these institutions to the control of the government, which may be at least as corrupt and self-serving. For example, they do not care for the quality of instruction and research in universities, or whether academics collect bribes for degrees. They care that the universities should promote the political line of the government and should not criticize it. Historians should delete inconvenient parts of the national historiographic narrative, while imposing a new partly fictional populist narrative, about tribal or national virtue and victimization. Control of higher education and research institutions can be further used to muzzle academically based public intellectuals by dismissing some and terrorizing others by threatening them with losing their livelihood. Outdated state media may need to be reformed, but not by being sold to a pro-government oligarch or by bringing in new management to turn a television channel into an instrument of populist and neo-illiberal propaganda.

Unmediated Politics

Ancient absolutist democracy was direct and unconstrained. Direct democracy was possible in small city-states
where virtually all the voters (the minority of the residents)
could gather in one place to debate and deliberate, or
listen to a demagogue and start a riot, as the case may be.
Face-to-face interactions and familiarity were necessary.
An assembly could turn into a mob when all decided to
pretend they had no personal identity. Anonymous mobs
then became responsible for individual actions. When
the mob anesthetized individual conscience and people
imitated each other's actions, pure passions dominated
and reason could not be bothered to awaken from its
induced slumber.

Classical style democratic mobs and demagogues disappeared from modern democracy together with face-to-face
city square politics. Consequently, in modern representative democracies, the political party came to mediate the
relations between leaders and followers. The mediation
moderated the populism of direct democracy because
the party had to reconcile different passions and interests
and come to compromises about policies and lists of
candidates that would appeal to different groups. (The
totalitarian party, such as the Communist, Nazi, or Ba'ath
parties, shares with democratic parties only the title of a
party, so I am ignoring it.)

Recently, though, after a couple of centuries of existence,
the political party has been losing its moderating and
mediating influence, along with political power. Zakaria
(2003) noted the return of direct democracy through the
development of constitutionally non-binding polls that
in fact bind elected politicians, who become hostages to
the temporary vagaries of popular opinions and passions
between elections. The introduction of party primary
elections encouraged classical extremism. Levitsky and
Ziblatt (2018) attributed the failures of political parties

to act as democracy's gatekeepers and keep populist and illiberal leaders out of elected office to open primaries that replaced elections controlled by party insiders in "smoke filled rooms," a historically fitting metaphor as the introduction of primaries happened at about the same time as the cancerous effects of tobacco products became known. Activists who tend to vote in primaries tend to be more passionate, more populist, than passive voters who cannot be bothered to vote.

Legislative and regulatory transparency that is effective for curbing corruption also creates opportunities for direct and immediate preemptive interventions by well-informed extremists, special interests, and lobbyists. Direct donations to candidates rather than to political parties, the influence of mass media oligarchs, and the effects of polling, reinforce each other's weakening effects on political parties, and the consequent modern rhyming with ancient direct democracy. The emergence of charismatic leaders with independent wealth and fame, sometimes based on their ancestry or family brand – "Kennedy," "Bush," "Clinton" – rather than on the backing of a recognized party brand is another symptom of the decline of the political party.

Old and neo-illiberals used extra-parliamentary plebiscites when they wanted to by-pass legislatures and representative democracy. Plebiscites are useful for manipulating the majority of the population by framing questions and offering bivalent choices so there can be only one obvious vote. Plebiscites can legitimize new constitutions or constituent assemblies that do not enjoy the support of a parliamentary majority. Bivalent choices exclude the possibility of compromise on the issue at hand or on a range of issues in larger policy tradeoffs. Plebiscites increase social polarization in a "winner takes all" majoritarian system that excludes minorities from decision making. The aggregation of all the results of plebiscites may be inconsistent (Sartori 1987, 115–120). Zakaria (2003) recorded the exponential rise in the number of plebiscites (including referenda, initiatives, and recalls) in the United States, especially in California, since 1975. The referenda were designed to directly by-pass politicians, special interests, and so on, but were financed by special interests and generated populist inconsistent results, since the citizens had inconsistent passions, to simultaneously reduce taxes and increase the level of public services. Political institutions in California retained responsibility with no political power. Californian representatives were left with discretionary powers over only 15 percent of the state's budget and little authority to reach decisions by debate, deliberation, and compromise. As Sartori (1987, 116) put it, referendum democracy is "an overkill," a "self-killing," and "suicidal" (283). Political self-destruction is populism in a nutshell.

Writing in 2003, before the American Supreme Court lifted limits on political donations by rich donors, Zakaria bemoaned the dependence of parties and politicians on constant fund raising from small donors. Politicians became obliged to maintain the stream of donations by satisfying many small donors. If they took unpopular positions, they could run out of funds immediately. This again has the effect of rhyming with classical direct illiberal democracy. Zakaria thought in 2003 that allowing a few mega donors to finance politics would solve this problem. He was wrong. Levitsky and Ziblatt (2018) attributed part of the decline in the powers of political parties to the opposite reason: mega-rich politicians like Berlusconi, Babiš, and Trump, who can pay for their own campaigns, and donors who remain in the background and under-write the campaigns of more charismatic leaders, while ignoring party elites. The third alternative that neither mentioned for party finance is for the state to finance parties according to the strength of their parliamentary representation. This form of finance favors old over new parties, and encourages crooks to get into politics in order to embezzle the state subsidies, yet it strengthens parties in representative democracies.

These trends toward classical direct democracy began in the 1970s. Social media accelerated such trends in the twenty-first century by enabling political leaders to connect directly with their base, bypassing local party organizations and the legacy media, as in the ancient assemblies. Consequently, it has become easier for leaders to take over weak political parties, as Orbán and Trump did, and rebrand them. When traditional political parties are weak and miss a "tribal" base, it is easier to start new parties on the basis of personal charisma, as did Fujimori, Berlusconi, the Kaczyński brothers, the demi-liberal populists Babiš and Kurz, and the liberal Macron.

Neo-illiberal democratic charismatic leaders do not need to distribute party patronage to connect with their followers. On the contrary, the party depends on the leader's special direct relation with voters to win elections. When the illiberal leader founds his own party as Berlusconi and Babiš did respectively in Italy and the Czech Republic, the leader selected party officials without a constituency of their own, sometimes former employees, who were politically and sometimes financially entirely dependent on him. When neo-illiberal leaders reconstituted preexisting political parties, as in Hungary, the United States, and Israel, the parties initially played a bigger role and patronage networks were significant, but became gradually feeble, and under the control of the leader. Israel's Netanyahu and Hungary's Orbán expelled from their parties leaders who had independent following of their own. Trump took over the Republican Party and turned it into a personalized party, where all the politicians are dependent on him and his special direct relationship with their voters, in an incredibly short time, faster and more thoroughly than Orbán or Netanyahu.

The public mass rally, as a tool of mobilization and manipulation, has been useful for ancient and modern demagogues to drum up and manipulate the passions of their followers, and silence their rational and critical faculties. In modern mass societies only small sections of the population can be accommodated in public spaces. Political communication had to be mediated through the mass media that centralized and controlled the communication process. Totalitarian regimes misused the centralization of the media to attempt to control the flow of information to their subjects, and determine their beliefs and values. Yet, in liberal democracies the centralization of the media allowed the reduction of public exposure to populist demagoguery and disinformation.

Since in modern societies the mobs cannot come to the demagogue, the demagogue comes to them. Neo-illiberal leaders have been holding passionate rallies, where the leader comes to the people, who are relieved of individuality and reason and are allowed to express their emotions via the leader, as populists have for centuries. Much has been written on Trump's rallies, but Modi's rallies in India are actually more revealing because of the habit of his supporters to wear masks bearing his face, thus explicitly abolishing their individuality to become one with their leader. The current pandemic will likely fully transition the mass rallies online, to complete a process that started with the invention of social media.

New information technologies, mostly social media, dismantled the barriers to direct communications from leader to followers. Social media reconstructed the ancient public square in cyber space, thereby weakening the power of the press to constrain politics. This was foreseen by some of the founders and early theoreticians of the internet. Yet, their image of the ancient agora as a place of rational deliberation was on the romantic margins of historiography. The agora was often a space where demagogues and mobs, protected by anonymity, could spread rumors, silence reason, eliminate personal responsibility, manipulate passions for political action, and hook up with others who shared their passions and mutually affirmed wishful beliefs that express those passions rather than reality. It was also a space for older men to chase boys, which is also unfortunately replicated in cyber space.

As in classical direct democracy, the neo-illiberal "leader" can develop a direct relation with atomized individuals who may together comprise a mob, through Twitter, at once, to millions. "Twitter ... is the closest thing we have to the democracy of the ancient world: fickle, violent, empowering. People have rediscovered the liberating effects of being able to gang up on individuals who have displeased them. It is exhilarating. And it can be deadly" (Runciman 2018, 142). As in a mob, an electronic "echo chamber" not only reinforces passions and the narrative representation of strong passions, but also augments them, as each echo is "louder," more passionate, and extremist than the one before, until it reaches a violent crescendo.

Media

Without informed citizenship, there can be no political accountability. Direct or indirect control of the media can disinform, misinform, and uninform voters. When the state owns the electronic mass media, as in Hungary and Poland, neo-illiberal governments abolish the independence of the state media to turn mass media into a platform for populist illiberal propaganda, to keep their viewers manipulated, afraid, threatened, and believing in their dependence on the protection of the neo-illiberals. When the mass media is private, the neo-illiberals pressure owners to sell their outlets to friendly owners, or bankrupt them to the same effect. In Italy, Berlusconi owned most of the commercial channels. In the Czech Republic, the prime minister owns the two quality daily newspapers. In Israel a friendly to the Likud Party American Republican billionaire, Sheldon Edelson, owns a free and hence *most printed* daily newspaper *Yisrael Hayom* (*Israel Today*). To gain control of the *most popular* daily newspaper in Israel *Yediot Acharonot* (*The Latest News*), Netanyahu offered its owner to limit the competition from *Yisrael Hayom* by enacting a special law, trading one loyal newspaper for another to achieve total control of the mass printed media, with the exception of *Haaretz*, the smaller circulation liberal daily. Netanyahu failed, and Israel's media remained mostly independent. In the United States, there is just one nominally private neo-illiberal television channel (FOX) that represents the government.

Neo-illiberals do not need to exercise total domination of the media typical of totalitarianism. They must only control the main media sources for their supporters to keep manipulating their passions. Neo-illiberals can safely ignore small circulation magazines and newspapers because nobody hears them when they scream. For this reason, unlike authoritarian regimes, they need not make use of libel laws to silence their opponents, though Trump made empty threats to change the libel laws. If there is still some independent mass media, like some of the print media in Poland, illiberal governments can use existing or new laws against defamation of officials or the state to silence and deter critics. But once there is no independent mass media left, this becomes redundant, as in Hungary.

When the mass media enjoys diverse private ownership, neo-illiberal leaders attempt to discredit it and bombard citizens with disinformation, not so much to convince as to confuse and disorient sufficiently for neutralizing the media as a check on their power. Scandals and transgressive speech can distract attention further from political reality. If enough people are confused and do not know who and what to believe, they will trust their passions, and believe articulated narratives expressions of those passions. For example, in Hungary, the ruling Fidesz used state resources to spread a fabricated "Soros Plan" to settle immigrants in Hungary, of all places. This fabrication was hatched by American political consultants and served to distract voters from the actual reality of constant demographic decline and emigration, while expressing anti-Semitic and xenophobic passions.

Independent free and private media flourished in the 1990s in post-Communist countries alongside public radio and television. After half a century of disinformation and propaganda, there was hunger for real news. Television was never entirely beyond the influence of political interests, but the public media aspired to and occasionally achieved the independence of the BBC. But the same financial economic challenges that undermined legacy media in established liberal democracies challenged even more media in poorer and smaller markets. Consequently, international publishing companies who saw their revenues fall when advertisers moved online and circulations declined, cut their staff and reduced their coverage, further decreasing circulation. Private media descended then into a death spiral. Local oligarchs then bought mass media firms for political rather than economic reasons, such as serving the illiberal governments in return for other favors.

The uniqueness of the populist neo-illiberal media is not in its partisanship. European print media has often been partisan in the sense that it *argued* mostly for a prescribed range of policies. For example, in the UK, the *Daily Telegraph* argued for opposite policies and values to those of the *Guardian* as *Le Figaro* and *l'Humanité* did in France, and *Al Hamishmar* ("For Zionism, Socialism, and the Brotherhood of Nations" on its masthead) differed from *Hatzophe* ("the newspaper of religiously observant Zionists") in Israel. Their readers knew that if they wanted to be exposed to alternative arguments, they should read more than one daily. When the *Independent* daily was founded by former *Daily Telegraph* editors in the UK, its innovative selling gimmick was pluralistic non-partisanship. As a sign of the times, the *Independent* was bought by a Russian oligarch who abolished its printed edition to save on the costs of printing and distribution.

The populist neo-illiberal media is unique in *not* arguing for anything. It by-passes reason to directly manipulate the passions, rather than appeal to interests and ideals. The populist media gives narrative form to the passions, most notably fear; it needs bogeymen to scare the readers who are already frightened, though they do not know of what.

Such a bogeyman may be real, like Iran for Netanyahu, or entirely fictional like George Soros' refugee plan for Hungary, imaginary waves of refugees in Central Europe, or a Ukrainian plot to help the American Democrats win the 2016 elections. Only the illiberal demagogue stands between the bogeyman and the frightened voters.

Nevertheless, when a real menace appeared in the form of a tiny but deadly virus, the illiberals were no good at protecting their people. Rather than rationally frighten or caution, they attempted, at least initially, to calm down and accustom their followers to the danger and the likely costs in human lives. They also attempted to spread the wishful thinking that a far more infectious and deadly virus than the viruses of the common flu was, in fact, just a kind of a flu that will make people sick and then go away. They did not want to assume responsibility for the inevitable downturn of the economy, or the deaths and sufferings, not just from the plague, but also from the breakdown of an overstretched medical system. They failed, not only because of brute medical reality, but also because demagogues who spent their political careers frightening people against often non-existing dangers, were not capable of instigating, controlling, and manipulating weaker emotions that may counter fear, like confidence and willingness to sacrifice for the greater good. The populist masses, who were used to having their fears encouraged, or even generated and then manipulated, did not know how to allow the same demagogues to manipulate them in the opposite direction, except in populist attacks on upper-middle-class "experts." The coronavirus plague lesson may or may not be retained by the populists who voted for illiberal democrats, as the costs in human lives, lost jobs, and collapsing economies accumulate. Traumas may deter, as they did after the Second World War, or they may be suppressed and eventually forgotten.

The media business model of appealing to passions, chiefly xenophobia and soft pornography, had preceded neo-illiberalism by a generation, and had previously flourished in the nineteenth century in Europe. After the Second World War it was reinvented by Rupert Murdoch in Australia, but gradually took over the globe. The internet has disrupted the financial foundation of the independent media by taking away much of its advertising revenues and reducing its circulation by offering free alternatives. The Neo-illiberal attacks on the media have been facilitated by the financial weakness of the legacy mass media. Neo-illiberal states can use their advertising budgets to keep media outlets afloat and offer "free" information to newspapers that cannot afford to hire journalists to cover all the news.

The information revolution has shortened effective messages to sound bites, and now to even shorter tweets, and even shorter symbols, emoji. Politicians started using Twitter with its 140-character limit (later doubled to verbose 280) because it won an audience of followers who did not want to read more than a sentence or two, and released them from the mediation of the media. The soundbite and Twitter impose on those who use them what used to be called a few technologies ago "telegraphic language." Ungrammatical sentences came to convey anti-elitist authenticity and honesty. This decadent political language is new, antithetical to the florid rhetoric of the ancients. "Friends, Romans, countrymen," would have taken already too many characters. Caesar and Cicero would have failed the test of Twitter. Emoji that express emotions: ☹ ☺ have returned language to its proto-literate archaic stage. This is politically significant because it is difficult, if not impossible, to use twits or emoji to pose arguments, or provide evidence, rather than to express populist passions. The media then is the populist message.

Disinformation

There is nothing new about disinformation. Politicians and state agencies have always been lying or telling half-truths to try to fashion beliefs that form the basis for political action. People tend not to believe information that comes from strangers who obviously stand to gain from convincing people to believe them. To be believed, disinformers spread *rumors* that are told by acquaintances rather than strangers and seem to come from nowhere in particular and everywhere in general. Spreading false rumors has been a tool of political warfare. This tool becomes particularly politically potent when ordinary people lose trust in experts, technocrats, and other authoritative sources of information. The disappearance of reliable sources of information creates a vacuum that rumors fill. The information vacuum has deepened and disinformation proliferated partly because there are fewer resources for the declining legacy media to fact check and conduct independent investigative reporting.

To understand why rumors are so effective and dangerous in spreading false beliefs we should take a short sojourn into epistemology, the theory of knowledge. Epistemology distinguishes five *and only five* types of sources of everything we know: *empirical* – from the senses (you see or hear this book); *rational* – from reason (you know that 32 + 32 = 64); *introspective* – from self-knowledge (you know how you feel now); *memory* (you remember where you bought this book); and *testimonial* – from what others tell you. To wit: Everything you and I know about Antarctica or the French Revolution is from testimonial sources, since we have not seen them with our own eyes, were not born with rational knowledge of them, they are not parts of us, and what we remember about them is *only* from testimonies of other people traceable to Antarctica or the French Revolution.

One way to acquire knowledge from testimonies is by evaluating their reliabilities. We learn to trust what some people or sources tell us and to distrust others, and over time we also learn to distinguish what we *want* people to tell us from their reliability. For example, I like to believe an email that promises me untold riches hidden in Nigeria, but I also know not to trust spam emails. Disinformation

attempts to derange our evaluation of testimonial reliabilities. It misrepresents reliable media repeatedly as
"lying" or "fake" news, while imitating reliable sources
in appearance, style, and format. If reliable and unreliable
testimonial sources become sufficiently indistinguishable,
people would trust neither and would be tempted to
choose between conflicting sources according to what they
already believe or like to believe, such as narrative expressions of their passions

Multiple *independent* testimonies can generate
knowledge even when testimonies are unreliable or when
their reliabilities cannot be estimated. For example,
suppose you ask me for a phone number of a restaurant I
recommend and I answer that I do not recall the number.
You ask me to take a guess and I blurt out the first seven-
digit number that comes into my mind when I hear the
restaurant's name. I add that you should not trust me on
this, since my intuition of the number is highly unreliable.
We can agree that neither of us *knows* the correct phone
number. But suppose you repeat the same exchange with
my dinner partner in that restaurant, who could not have
overheard our conversation and the number I blurted out.
But she repeats the same number. Irrespective of our self-
attested unreliability in this matter, the probability that
we agreed on that number by coincidence is 0.0000001^2.
You still need to eliminate the possibility that we played a
practical joke on you, or that we repeated unconsciously
some phone number that had nothing to do with the
restaurant such as the neighborhood Chinese takeaways
but, otherwise, you gained knowledge that the testifiers
themselves did not possess. We perform this kind of
computation numerous times every day, especially when
we learn something that is not obvious from strangers;
usually, without being aware of it. We look for coherent
independent testimonies that have low prior probability, are
surprising, and informative. Historians, detectives, jurists,
and journalists make such inferences from independent
testimonies for a living (Tucker 2016).

Disinformers spread rumors to bombard people with coherent disinformation from all directions, *to appear as if dependent testimonies with a single deceptive source are independent.* Mixing the deceptive content with some independently verifiable information serves to increase the reliability of the disinformation. Historically, such spreading of rumors had the snail pace of face-to-face social interactions. Now, spreading rumors has become as quick as a click on a keyboard. Information technology mechanically turbo-charges the rumor mills to bombard social media with dependent testimonies that appear to come from nowhere in particular but everywhere in general. Before social media, this could only be done by implanting gossip in select different groups, orally, in person, to make it difficult for anybody to trace the rumors back to any single source. The victims of disinformation would hear coherent rumors from many people and even repeat them themselves, so the rumors appeared to come from everywhere with no identifiable source.

Social media's rumor-mongering capacities are significantly augmented by technologically facilitated pervasive anonymity. Gossips, shills, bots, and simply crazy people are all protected from accepting responsibility for deliberate disinformation by cyber anonymity. Consumers of rumors cannot trace them back to their sources or find out if they are independent. Intelligence analysts, respectable journalists, and historians, trace the origins of information for a living. It is no coincidence that the reliabilities of these groups of people, intelligence analysts, serious journalists, and historians are now particularly under neo-illiberal attack. They get in the way of spreading disinformation.

The algorithms of social media, especially Facebook, are not comparable to the proverbial person who screams "fire!" in a crowded theater. Social media does not even quite hand the "fire!" screamer a megaphone. Social media is rather in the position of a person who sends a phone text message that says "fire!" to exactly the group of theatergoers who are most likely to believe it, panic, and resend it to more people. When facts cannot be distinguished from disinformation in a global social media hall of distorted testimonial mirrors that reflect each other, social media technologies, in the hands of well-trained and vast army of trolls, are fast becoming weapons of mass delusion.

Populism as Wishful Thinking

The strength of the populist political passions that silence reason and sustain neo-illiberal democracy is manifested in "post-truth," a new word for the much older concept "wishful thinking," the construction of beliefs as narrative manifestations of strong passions. When people trust their passions, their gut feelings, rather than their senses and reason they become disoriented. As Paul Veyne (quoted in Elster 1999, 346) put it, "beliefs born of passion serve it badly." Blatant populist lying demonstrates the strong passions that generate credibility among those who trust their passions more than their senses and reason. Blatant lying may also generate a sense of solidarity among all those who share passions and their narrative expressions as a mutually reinforced collective delusion. The passionate disinforming narrative can be told straight, or it can be implied by decontextualizing and then reframing true statements. For example, when media outlets tell a story about a criminal and identify him as an immigrant while not identifying comparable criminals as natives, they fit reality to a wishful thinking passionate xenophobic narrative. Vice versa, when the media ignores the fact that almost all random mass shooting in the United States has been committed by native white males, they eliminate challenges to the passionate xenophobic narrative. The populist American reaction to the coronavirus pandemic, wishing it away, denying the need for quarantine and social distance that have severe economic costs, demonstrated the distance of wishful thinking from reality, at unprecedented speed and at a great cost. Nevertheless, the illiberals and authoritarians will attempt to fit this calamity to a xenophobic scapegoating narrative that may fit the wishful thinking of at least some of their followers, just as they had during previous plagues in previous centuries. Conspiracy theories may then be used and manipulated to transfer responsibility from illiberals in power to scapegoats.

Disinformation becomes particularly effective when its targets desire self-deception. Since populism, as I define it, is founded on strong political passions, powerful disinformation is founded on manipulating the same populist passions. Our strongest emotions, especially under stress, are fear, anger, hate, and anxiety. These emotions can override reason, an evolutionarily later and sometimes weaker mental force. The imaginative faculties of some of the victims of disinformation are poorer than those of disinformation specialists who recycle narratives that express those emotions as virtual reality. It takes some talent for self-deception not to be amazed at the incredible coincidence that each and every politician who challenged Putin's aspirations and policies turns out to be a gay freemason pedophile in cahoots with immigrant Moslem rapists and the Jewish George Soros! It is even more amazing that this world-wide conspiracy keeps spreading to include more and more politicians. If you do not believe me, just read it on social media, share and like!

Most people know that it is impossible to lead a debauched life and yet have a strong loving family. It is impossible to be repeatedly bankrupt and yet be a multibillionaire. We know it is impossible to vulgarly deride and offend most of humanity and still be respected and project soft power. We may even realize that it is impossible to improve public services for retirees in societies in demographic decline without young working immigrants. However, if the trade-offs that reality forces on us were avoidable, it would be great to live in a convincing populist fantasy land, a virtual unreality TV show. On TV, it is possible to have the cake and still eat it, while losing weight.

Historically, before television, the narratives that contained impossible contradictions were *myths*. In the modern world we rationalize our myths. Public relations experts, spinners, biased journalists, and so on, are the new myth makers and tellers. They do not invent or initiate the inner contradictions. But once they are generated, they attempt to systematize them, make them look coherent with each other in a master narrative. They are not quite new Homers, but more like the editors of the *Iliad* who put various myths together and strove for consistency that eluded them.

Left to its own devices, critical reason may trump passions and self-deceptive wishful thinking. *Mutual deception* serves then to suppress reason. If I lie to you and you lie to me in a cyber echo chamber, we may come to believe in things so ridiculous that we would be unable individually to deceive ourselves about. This was Václav Havel's analysis of ideology in *The Power of the Powerless,* a mean for self-deception that preserves our sense of personal worth. This is how mass rallies have been working, at least since the ancient Greeks, to silence reason and let the passions generate beliefs. Social media networks and algorithms added a new advanced techno-logical augmenting aspect to it, LIKE! We no longer need to stand in large public spaces to listen to a demagogue and cheer him and each other to deceive each other, we can do so from the comfort of our own smart phone, SHARE and LIKE! The social media echo chamber augments extremism and wishful thinking when each participant eggs on the others until they settle on the most passionate extreme version of whatever they started with and LIKE it!

The biblical God is said to have created the world through his word. Authoritarian and neo-illiberal leaders stake a claim to such divine power. They create a virtual world through their disinforming word. They expect to generate facts merely by uttering them. The imposition of a blatantly nonsensical, internally incoherent, but emotionally consistent and satisfying narratives manifests their power. The more preposterous is the narrative the more authentic and powerful is the leader. The rise of "reality television" as a political force that blurs the distinction between spontaneous and carefully scripted narrative, between fiction and reality, is the modern creation though the word. The same is true for carefully scripted wrestling matches. Trump emerged from the demi-monde of televised blurred fiction masquerading as reality, as a secular televangelist, an economics faith healer, and above all, a "reality show" star. Fornicating televangelists and faith healers, exposed by journalists as wearing earplugs to receive information from associates about what ails their supplicants, in order to appear to have miraculous knowledge, did not lose the faith of their followers because of those brute facts. The faithful were too desperate to believe to accept reality. In reality shows and soap operas "reality" is scripted and can be changed at will, even at the cost of internal narrative inconsistency. Viewers who adopt their world view from these genres may not quite distinguish virtual from reality. Then, a White House apologist can talk with a straight face about having "alternative facts," as Kellyanne Conway did. Trump expects to create reality for his followers by uttering it, just as populist leaders of post-Communist countries conjure a Moslem refugee invasion by their word, in countries with just a few hundred refugee applications each year. The imposition of mythical narratives on politics was common in the ancient world. Caesar, for example, was surrounded by myths that he may have encouraged if not invented.

Populist neo-illiberalism's idea of truth is *emotivist*; true is what populists feel strongly about. Truth, history, politics, and public opinions are, then, just narrative expressions of passions. For example, if a populist really dislikes Hillary Clinton, then she must be running a pedophile ring from a pizza shop in Washington. This is exactly the kind of myth the ancients were telling about each other. For example, if a person feels helpless, afraid, and without control over their destiny, it can be put in narrative form as a conspiracy involving alien lizards, Masons, and Jewish financiers who control the world; the ancients would have spoken about gods and demons. Anybody who tells a different story must be a part of a conspiracy to market alternative "faked" narratives. Their fakery is not in lack of correspondence with some reality but in having different, wrong, emotions.

Populist historiography is not about evidence for the past but about the identity and emotions of those who author it. The emotivist theory of historical truth is embarrassingly close to some philosophies of historiography that do not distinguish historiographic narratives from fiction and reduce historical truth to power relations and other biases. They are oddly consistent with this aspect of populism, even though there is not much mutual appreciation and support between the two groups. If passions decide, the reception of historiographic narratives, fear, hate, blaming scapegoats and avoiding responsibility will be a tough act to follow with tolerance, compassion, empathy, and care.

Unlike during earlier outbreaks of populism, authoritarianism, and totalitarianism, at least for now, there are no significant intellectual inspirations, legitimizations, or fellow travelers for neo-illiberalism and only a few for populism, no Heidegger or Gentile, De Man, or Merleau-Ponty. The Alt-Right ideology and label was invented by an intellectual with a politics degree from Yale, Paul Gottfried. But this may go to prove that even for their name and ideology, white supremacists required the services of an intellectual who grew up ultra-Orthodox, and whose first degree is from Yeshiva University. Formerly conservative journals like the *National Review* and the *National Interest* have already become ideological apologists for populist neo-illiberalism or are in the process of becoming so. But most intellectuals may have learned the historical lessons, though it is more likely that since contemporary populism is more anti-intellectual than anti- anything else, intellectuals are not wanted.

Populist *emotivist* historiography is distinct from totalitarian historiography that simply denied well-documented historical reality. The totalitarians accepted the idea of objective historical truth, but denied that there was a Holocaust, or that Stalin's secret police murdered millions, or that some Bolshevik former leaders ever walked the earth, especially in the company of Lenin or Stalin. Populist historiography does not deny. Instead, it relativizes. The Holocaust, then, is yet another narrative about history that is politically motivated and is true for people with strong emotions about it. SS veterans may offer an alternative narrative that they feel strongly about. There are no higher criteria for choosing between them, so we can either tell all the stories, or pay attention only to our own, not because it is superior, but because it is ours. The neo-illiberal populist strategy is to drown any truth in a Niagara Fall of alternative narratives, so the untrained and uneducated would be unable to decide between these alternatives on objective grounds. The choice should be made, then, on the grounds of passions and politics. The passions of the populists are stronger than those of liberals and reality and evidence be damned.

Historical Amnesia and Sisyphean Politics

For the historically educated, observing much of contemporary politics resembles having to watch repeatedly a bad horror movie. As Wynne McLaughlin, put it, "maybe history wouldn't have to repeat itself if we listened once in a while."

The ancient pioneers of democracy had short democratic histories to draw lessons from. The rhetorical style of historiography that the Greeks and Romans practiced was designed for pedagogical purposes. It resembled "docudramas," in mixing reality with fiction. The historians attempted to teach what would have been best said in historical circumstances, rather than what was actually said, to teach exemplary best practices. Such historiography is better at forming ideal examples than at drawing lessons from past mistakes.

Today, we can take advantage of an additional couple of centuries of global democratic historical experience to learn from. Still, even with well-documented historical records, it is possible to repeat the same old mistakes as if democracy has no history, if only a few people are familiar with the historical record. Historical "amnesia" allows the repetition of socially forgotten mistakes. Without studying historiography (writings about history) each generation would "forget" what it neither experienced nor was retold by its elders. History cannot by itself prevent its own repetition. Personal historical memory can stretch back as long as two generations or so, but no longer. According to this "two generations memory rule," the political reactions of democracies to the global recession in the 1930s and to the menace of totalitarianism have simply receded behind the historical horizon.

Often, state schools teach "history" in the genre of "great people and events in national history," that suppresses, instead of stresses, mistakes and close calls. It also ignores what happened globally to the ancestors of *other* people as a result of their mistakes and the mistakes of others. In Western European countries like France and Germany, and in Israel, which experienced the previous catastrophe most acutely, not to say traumatically, formal education systems attempt to pass on relevant historical knowledge about mistakes made before the Second World War, but classic Greek and Roman histories are taught only to a select few students. The UK and the United States made mistakes in the 1930s, but they did not result in domestic catastrophe comparable to that of continental Europe. They also did not undergo the experience of occupation in the Second World War. Consequently, without major traumas and with a sense of victorious heroism, there was little or no intergenerational transmission of historical lessons other than pride. Post-totalitarian societies in Central and Eastern Europe failed to come to terms with their pasts, both on a personal level – families rarely discuss the historical past – and on a national level, by ending history instruction with the Second World War, and avoiding public discussions of totalitarianism and collaboration. The results are not just the recurrence of repressed and then forgotten populist and illiberal ideologies, movements, policies, and disasters, but also the repetition of tactical mistakes by those who oppose illiberalism but did not learn its history. For example, it should not have surprised British prime minister Cameron that a plebiscite, a classical weapon in the illiberal arsenal since Napoleon, delivered a populist result.

"Those who cannot remember the past are condemned to repeat it," George Santayana famously wrote in his 1905 book *The Life of Reason*. Santayana sought to articulate an Aristotelean *via media* virtue of historical consciousness, between historical amnesia and life in historical trauma. He warned against becoming prisoners of traumatic historical experiences and continuously living and reliving them obsessively by repetitively reacting to new historical experiences as if they were the old traumatic ones. Continuous adaptation is the price of historical and personal longevity. Not every authoritarian in power with wicked heir is Adolf the Second, not every agreement with a dictator is a reenactment of appeasement and the Munich Accords, but also not every humanitarian intervention abroad is a new "Iraq."

Santayana thought that historical progress and personal maturity result from learning from experience: When individuals or nations remember their mistakes, they do not repeat them. When we consider what we could have done better in the past, we do things better in the future. When historical experience is not retained, the results are permanent political and personal infancy. Historically amnesiac individuals and societies then make mistakes typical of children or societies with short histories, because they have little experience to draw on.

Democratic theorists, at least since Thomas Jefferson and John Stuart Mill, have warned that democracy can thrive only when voters are educated, possessing historical virtue in Santayana's sense. An educated citizenship is the "infrastructure" of democracy. Scolding populists for being historically ignorant when they are in the grip of powerful passions, fear, anxiety, and personal insecurity is too late, useless, or even arrogantly counterproductive.

Today's populist neo-illiberalism expresses milder versions of passions and policies that failed in the past two centuries, leading to two world wars and the deepening of the economic depression of the 1930s: Blocking international trade routes and breaking production chains through barriers and tariffs, closing borders to refugees and risking taking entrepreneurial economic migrants, and scapegoating ethnic and religious minorities for economic difficulties. A Europe of truly independent nation-states will restore the great-power politics of the nineteenth century. The largest country, Russia, will emerge strongest from renationalizing geopolitics.

Populism was not supposed to happen. During the twentieth century, humanity subjected itself to a painful learning process by trying extreme new ideologies. The extreme right led to the catastrophe of the Second World War. The extreme left collapsed with the Soviet Bloc in 1989. At the end of the Cold War, Francis Fukuyama argued that humanity had learned the lessons from its history, and, by elimination, only liberal democracy was left standing at the philosophical end of history. A minor assumption in Fukuyama's reasoning was that when societies make historical mistakes, they learn, retain the lessons, and pass them from generation to generation, and to other societies who did not participate in the historical experience, so nobody would have to relearn the lessons the hard way.

Fukuyama did not examine the possibility that societies might not retain knowledge and lessons from failed historical experiments and then might unwittingly repeat them. Societies devoid of historical consciousness are condemned inevitably to *"Sisyphean politics,"* following the ancient Greek (and Camus' existentialist) myth about King Sisyphus, who spends eternity rolling a huge boulder up a mountain. When he reaches the top of the mountain, the boulder rolls down. Sisyphus must roll it up the mountain yet again eternally. Without historical memory and consciousness, societies may retry the same failed ideologies and policies that lead to disaster, inevitably, again and again, in endless cycles. They must keep rolling that illiberal democratic boulder up the political mountain yet again, until it inevitably rolls back into the authoritarian abyss, carrying with it the populist illiberals who pushed it.

Some of the resistance to populism and neo-illiberalism in continental Europe today benefits from lingering traumatic memories of previous experiments with populism and illiberalism before and during the Second World War. A comparison of the demographics of the supporters of Trump, Brexit, and France's Le Pen is instructive: Statistically they have higher support among the less educated and the rural as opposed to urban, educated, and professional voters. Yet, there is a huge gap in the support for populism and illiberalism among the over-65 demographic. Older French voters who remember Pétain, Laval, and the Nazi occupation, or lived sufficiently close to those events to receive and retain the then recent memories of others, are the least populist illiberal voters in France; they do not vote for the National Front. Stockemer et al. (2018, 576–577) found, in general, a weak correlation between young age and voting for extreme right-wing parties in Europe. The category of extreme right wing has a narrower scope than populist illiberal in general; Forza Italia and the Czech ANO for example are populist illiberal but not extreme right wing. Still, extreme right wing is more closely connected ideologically with the failed ideologies of the first half of the twentieth century that young people do not remember, but older Europeans do.

Neo-Illiberalism is not Neo-Nationalist

For a historically amnesiac movement, populist neo-illiberalism is curiously accused of continuity with a long historical tradition, nationalism. Many commentators consider populist neo-illiberalism as a type of nationalism or simply nationalistic. I do not see continuity between nineteenth-century nationalism and present populist neo-illiberalism. *Nationalists wanted to help those they considered their own people first. Xenophobes want to hurt those whom they consider others first.* Nationalism and xenophobia do not contradict each other, but they are distinct. Populist neo-illiberalism is purely xenophobic. The most obvious example is Italy's Northern League, which has always been populist and xenophobic, though for most of its existence it was anti-nationalist in the most radical sense possible, denying the existence of an Italian nation and advocating the breakup of the state into its regional parts. The smooth transition from anti-nationalism to apparent Italian nationalist ideology demonstrates that xenophobic populism operates on a different and more fundamental level.

Apart from distinguishing an "in group" from "out groups," populist neo-illiberalism has none of the classical properties of nationalism: Some populist neo-illiberal movements are not statist but believe in deregulation and privatization. Nor do they believe that the state is the embodiment of the national spirit in time. There is no communitarian patriotic aspect to populist neo-illiberalism. It displays no altruism toward members of the in-group, no nation-state building through volunteering, no collection and construction of a national literature, no promotion of literary language, no construction of a historiography (except in Poland and perhaps Hungary), and no intellectual effort to generate national high culture that would be disseminated through a system of universal education. Traditionally, nationalism appealed to young people and often was idealistic. Nationalism worshipped youth, athleticism, and often militarism. The populist neo-illiberal "grey revolution" is anti-idealist and has nothing romantic about it.

Nationalists and neo-illiberals share nostalgic fantasies. But the nationalists appeal to collective history. The populist neo-illiberals typically do not have historical memories that are older than themselves. In Hungary and Poland, populists refer positively to pre-Second-World-War authoritarianism, without knowing much about that period after years of Communist disinformation and ignorance. Nationalist leaders were often poetic romantic intellectuals, who fantasized about becoming warriors and prophets, and occasionally fulfilled the first fantasy. Neo-illiberal leaders are either rich men or professional politicians. Neither can be suspected of writing poetry in their spare time about warriors and prophets. They do not advocate altruistic campaigns for national unity by mutual aid, or for volunteering to help the poor and educate the ignorant. Younger neo-illiberals do not rush to volunteer for military service or to form private militias. They may attack poor immigrants occasionally or go to the border looking for their ghosts, but they are too undisciplined to form a fighting force. They are too modern to give up on their individualism and form a small part in a larger collective, let alone contemplate sacrificing themselves for the collective. Populist neo-illiberal-democratic leaders do not try to block opportunities for corruption in the absence of rule of law. Nineteenth-century nationalist leaders were rarely corrupt. To take an Israeli example, can anybody imagine Theodore Herzl or David Ben Gurion demanding expensive cigars and pink champagne as remuneration for services rendered, as prime minister Netanyahu did?! Even in India, where the BJP is identified often as a "Hindu nationalist" party, the emphasis is on exclusion of Moslems. "Hinduism" is not a nation in the traditional sense, it includes diverse ethnic groups who speak different languages and have different cultures. There is a Hindu religion and culture, but the BJP is not interested in excluding other religions such as Buddhism or Jainism, but only in the Moslem minority.

The classical nineteenth-century self-definition of nationalism was founded on *language* with or without an ethnicity. Nationalists labored tirelessly to codify their national tongues and generate high culture in the vernacular. Linguistic fluency and literacy were hallmarks of national identity that distinguished the national in-group from outsiders. If people the nationalists considered "outsiders" had better command of the language and culture than members of the "in-group," nationalists either accepted them, as in France, or considered them dangerous infil-trators or impostors, as eventually in Germany. By contrast, neo-illiberal leaders need not know their mother tongue fluently, and certainly not literally. Illiberal voters, for example in the United States, may even interpret inarticulateness, limited vocabulary, and bad grammar and syntax as marks of authenticity that distinguish populist leaders from literate elites. The neo-illiberal populists may interpret high culture – knowledge of literature and history – as signaling elite non-technical education, and hence condescension and exclusion. There are no populist artistic or humanistic cultural expressions of "the people" and their folk-lore, as in classical nationalism, because populism, unlike nationalism, detests intellectuals.

Neo-illiberal xenophobic hostility is not limited to members of other nations. They can be hostile to any minority that can be distinguished somehow on any ground, including "traitorous" co-nationals. Neo-illiberals construct differences in order to create minorities that can be scapegoated for any number of reasons and no reason. The only basic necessary requirement is that they are weak minorities who cannot punch back. A telling sign is that none of the current populist xenophobic ire in Europe is directed at stereotypically rich foreigners; for example Russian oligarchs or South and East Asians, Indians, Vietnamese, Japanese, and Koreans. Hate is reserved for weaker Western Asians, who are typically poorer and do not have wealthy or powerful states to protect them. In East Europe there are actually more South and East Asians than West Asians because there are more joint ventures or direct investments there than Arabs, who pass through but do not wish to find refuge in post-Communist countries.

Indian populist neo-illiberalism has indeed ethno-nationalist and religious contents that are largely absent from the developed world's merely xenophobic neo-illiberalism. Since its founders defined the Indian state as constitutionally secular, at least in the sense of treating all religions equally, attacks on secularism are also attacks on liberal-secular institutions and the secular rule of law. Hindu ethno-nationalism and political theologies preceded the emergence of populist neo-illiberalism. The neo-illiberals, then, integrated these pre-existing religious and nationalist ideologies into their new populist and neo-illiberal agenda.

Populist neo-illiberalism is not Judeo-Christian, even in its most conservative senses. The Judeo-Christian scriptures are emphatically and unambiguously supportive of immigrants and promote solidarity among humans, and especially co-religionists. The Latin American migrants to North America are all Christian. The populist illiberal leaders are not typically religious (with the exception of Poland) – sometimes, as in the case of Trump, blatantly so. Some religious leaders outside Poland are too weak to preach to their dwindling congregants, fearing they may lose even more of them. So, they follow them out of the church into the public square to sanctify the demagogue, much as Aaron sanctifies the golden calf, hoping to buy time until Moses finally gets off that mountain and takes charge.

Neo-Illiberalism is not an Over-Reaction to Immigration

Another attempt to characterize populist illiberalism is as a reaction, or over-reaction, of authoritarians to rising levels of immigration. Stenner and Haidt (2018) inferred an authoritarian social "constant," of about a third of the electorate measured by the values parents wish to impart to children. Levitsky and Ziblatt (2018) estimated historically the authoritarian electoral base in the US at about 40 percent. By contrast, Norris and Inglehart (2019) argued against an authoritarian constant. They correlated authoritarian values with historical periods and generational cohorts, the younger the cohort, the less authoritarian. All the cohorts, though, became more authoritarian following the 2008 recession. Whatever are the authoritarian values and whether or not they have been constant in populations, it is obvious that authoritarians did not seriously challenge liberal democracy in most advanced industrial democracies between the end of the Second World War and the second decade of the twenty-first century. There were occasional waves of right-wing extremism in Europe, most notably of the National Front in France, but they never won elections and participated only in the Austrian governing coalition.

Stenner and Haidt (2018) were right, then, to argue that authoritarian values are *insufficient* for predicting populist or illiberal voting. To explain what turned authoritarians into illiberal voters, they added a variable they designated "normative threat," a vague concept associated with pluralist threats to "sameness" or "oneness," which they associated with "immigration." Authoritarians may encounter in the countryside few or no immigrants, but feel threatened by the end of perceived ethnic homogeneity and hegemony. Authoritarians can live with liberal democracy as long as they are not "triggered" by becoming aware of the existence of difference, albeit somewhere far,

in the big cities where people who look different, have
different language or mores, and so on, roam the streets.
This awareness drives them to political extremes. Liberals
and democrats should be careful then not to push their
buttons, or they go politically c-r-a-z-y and burn down
the democratic neighborhood and the liberal club. Norris
and Inglehart (2019) agreed that authoritarian values by
themselves do not explain neo-illiberal democracy and
that an additional new factor had to trigger the response.
Their favorite triggering factor however is not immigrants,
but liberals: that is, the imminent demographic dilution
of authoritarian or conservative demographics by legally
residing or native liberal population. The threat they
identified is not so much from legal immigrants as from
native multi-cultural, multi-ethnic, gender equal, sexually
tolerant, and younger liberals replacing their baby boomer
elders. At the moment of the turning of the demographic
tide, the old authoritarians make a last foray out of their
bunkers.

It is difficult to test these conflicting hypotheses, despite
the impressive statistical apparatus and regression analysis,
because it is difficult to measure empirically the concepts
they use in different senses. They refer to subjective mental
states that are weakly correlated with measurable social
reality. What is considered immigration, or more generally
"a threat to sameness," or just "liberal mores," are social
constructs that exist entirely inside the heads of those who
experience them. "Normative threats" exist only in the
particularly narrow spaces between some ears. What some
people consider a threat to sameness, others may consider
more of the same. There is simply no fact of the matter.

The empirical inadequacy of Stenner and Haidt's
conclusion is acknowledged by the authors when they
shift midway their reasoning from data and statistical
analysis to: "Common sense and historical experience"
that "tell us that there is some rate of newcomers into
any community that is too high to be sustainable – that
can overwhelm or even damage the host and make things

worse for both old and new members" (2018, 213). The histories of countries and states like Singapore, Israel, Australia, the United States, and Canada demonstrate that the majorities of people who live in a country or state can be immigrants without damaging or overwhelming natives or immigrants, as long as the immigrants are not colonialists or occupiers who wish to dominate and expropriate, rather than work, trade, and exchange.

Massive immigration to places like Israel (that doubled its population around 1950), or Canada, was reasonably successful without driving authoritarians off the wall, or off to build a wall, though immigrant groups to those countries shared practically nothing ethnically, culturally, or linguistically with each other, or with the older population. Jewish immigrants to Israel from Yemen or Libya had close to nothing in common with immigrants from Poland or Germany. They looked different, they had different religious practices, and many Europeans were socialist atheists; they had no common language, no common culture, and had different approaches to modernity. There was discrimination by East European Jews against Asian and African Jews. Their blocked mobility contributed to the rise of the Likud as the party of recent immigrants, and later to populism. Israeli populism, interestingly, is of more recent immigrants against older elite immigrant groups.

People have defined a foreigner or an immigrant radically differently in different regions and periods. Place of birth may have legal significance for citizenship laws of some countries. Ethnicity may be significant in other countries that recognize *jus sanguinis*. But, for most people, the conceptualization of member of the in-group versus the other is entirely constructed subjectively and is constantly shifting. Anybody and nobody can be constructed or deconstructed as a foreign threat or as a member of the in-group. For example, Czechs voted for a Slovak centrist populist billionaire, who speaks Czech with an accent, for prime minister. He rails against immigration. Czech

neo-Fascists voted for a racist party led by a quarter
Japanese, quarter Korean, half Czech "Dragons' Den"
reality show judge, named Okamura. They obviously did
not consider Okamura a foreigner or an immigrant, though
he looks Asian. By contrast, Hungarian authoritarians,
with the help of American consultants, constructed George
Soros, a Hungarian native who speaks fluent Hungarian
and is physically indistinguishable from anybody else in
Hungary, has invested many millions in liberating his
compatriots from Communism and helping their higher
education, including sending their populist prime minister
to study at Oxford University, as the ultimate "other." The
shameless American consultants who invented the foreign
bogeyman Soros were of Jewish descent and one of them
was openly gay and married to another man. They were
obviously not perceived as a foreigner threat.

The arbitrariness of what is and is not considered a
foreign "normative threat" to homogeneity was most
obvious in the Nazi order for Jews to wear yellow star
badges on their clothes, during the previous round of
authoritarian xenophobia in Europe. The obvious reason
was that there was absolutely nothing else to distinguish
them physically, linguistically, or culturally from other
Germans. The "normatively threatened authoritarians"
had to construct them as "normative threats" by forcing
them to wear badges that identified them as threateningly
different. Today, in the ethnically homogenous states
of East-Central Europe, authoritarians had to imagine
a phantasmagoric absent presence, invading hordes of
immigrant Moslems led by the Jewish Soros, in the absence
of any objectively existing real "normative threat."

In Poland and the Czech Republic, non-Russian Slavs
from other countries are not foreign. There are probably
millions of Ukrainians and former Yugoslavs living and
working in those countries, but they are not "immigrants."
The fear of the non-existing Moslem immigrants improved
the status of Vietnamese Czechs, who came to work in the
country during late Communism and stayed. They used to

be foreign immigrants. Now, not so much. In the whole of East Europe the most alienated and discriminated against minority are the native Roma (Gypsies), who have lived there since the Middle Ages and were decimated in the Holocaust. They are considered to have dark skin. In North America, Roma are considered white and are identified by their countries of origins, as Romanian, Slovak and so on. About twenty years ago, Czech television broadcast a documentary about Czech Roma families living ordinary middle-class lives in Canada. A few weeks later, Canada felt like it had to reimpose visa restrictions on all Czech citizens.

Americans mind Moslems, but they really dislike Christians from Latin America. Americans in coastal cities consider evangelical Christians with different values as their immigrant other, while they are fine with Mexicans. Upper-class Americans do not mind non-whites or foreign languages, but they may consider graduates of public colleges the other with whom they would not socialize or marry. The "rules" that distinguish the "ins" and "outs" change, and depend in many cases on the appearance of another more different group that in effect expands the in-group. Arguably, immigration from Mars will resolve all ethnic problems on Earth and turn all humans into members of the in-group.

These constructs do not reflect an objective reality that can be analyzed as a cause of illiberalism. The objects of xenophobia do not always exist but are always reflections of the states of mind of those who project their fears onto objects that are too weak to peel off the labels others stick on them; sometimes because they do not exist but are hallucinatory ghosts, like the Moslem invaders of Poland and Hungary. Immigration and liberals do not cause illiberalism and populism. Rather, xenophobia, fear in general, is projected onto immigrants or liberals, if they exist, or on ghosts, if they do not exist. *Immigrants do not cause xenophobia. It is xenophobia that constructs foreigners, immigrants, and other "others."* The question then is why the illiberals are afraid, what puts them in that state of mind in the first place? To take an extreme analogous example, if we want to understand Nazi anti-Semitism, studying Jewish communities and the history of German-Jewish relations is futile. The question is what put the Nazis in that pathological state of mind? Whatever the answer is, has nothing to do with who the Jews were or what they did, because they were constructed rather than discovered.

It is told that when the soldiers of the Red Army reached the suburbs of Berlin in 1945 and entered big houses with running hot water and sewage systems, Biedermeier furniture, Meissen porcelain and so on, they reacted by saying something like "They live like this, and they came to occupy us?!" The Red Army soldiers missed that the Germans did not occupy the East to get rich, though some did plunder the little that was there. Similarly, the correlation between immigrants and neo-illiberalism (illiberalism as such is not particularly hostile to immigration – illiberal countries in Latin America and the Caribbean attempted to attract immigrants) has another explanation than simple causal mechanism from the first to the second. Migration and refugees did not cause the crisis that resulted in populism and illiberalism. The crisis preceded them. Populist xenophobia and illiberalism are symptoms of deeper pathologies that preceded the refugee crisis and were then projected onto hapless refugees. Had there been no refugees and no migrants, as in Poland and Hungary, they would have been projected onto some other constructed weak minority or on imaginary creatures like extraterrestrial lizards in human form, as the Alt-Right myth goes.

Neo-Illiberalism is not Confused Socialism

The populist temptation in every democracy is to overheat the economy, create a temporary "high," inflate an asset bubble. One of the simplest methods is to lower interest rates. Banks, firms, and individuals then borrow more, invest, create jobs, and the economy grows. However, when the interest rates are too low, they generate inflation, lower incentives for saving, push investors into speculative ventures for lack of safer investment options with reasonable returns, and the Central Bank loses a powerful Keynesian lever on the economy should a recession necessitate it, and history proves that recessions are sooner or later inevitable. The historically recent solution has been the introduction of an independent central bank that sets interest rates without political interference. Democratically elected politicians decide on other economic policies, most significantly on fiscal policy, taxes, and spending.

Populist neo-illiberals wish to reverse that independence to control interest rates, to reduce them and keep them low. They can try to do that by regaining control over the Central Bank, or by pressuring its directors by reducing or increasing their salaries, or by publicly pressuring them, as Trump has been doing via Twitter.

But, apart from the rejection of the independence of the Central Bank, there is little in common between the economic policies of neo-illiberals that may be located on the standard left–right continuum: France's National Front has a socialist economic agenda, Hungary is running a crony capitalist economy, Trump at least appears to like tariffs and control or managed international trade while deregulating the economy and reducing taxes for the rich, Modi's BJP advocates deregulation like Trump, but also cuts to subsidies and welfare. The Swiss and Dutch populist neo-illiberals advocate some libertarian economic policies (though not free immigration, of course). There is little or nothing in common about the populist neo-illiberal economic policies. Stockemer et al. (2018, 276) attributed the absence of clear correlation between extreme right-wing voting patterns and unemployment or type of vocation to the different economic policies of extreme right-wing parties.

I found some negative correlation between populist neo-illiberal economic policies and the policies that preceded them: In India, the Congress party's corrupt state management of the economy led to a free market backlash. Since managed care was the Obama administration's signature policy, Trump has been seeking to abolish it. Fidesz and PiS in Hungary and Poland reacted against the free market ideology of the transition away from Communism with subsidies and government patronage. Since Israel's Netanyahu transitioned to a populist neo-illiberal in the middle of his premiership, after earlier advocating free market reforms and deregulation, he did not change the general direction of his economic policies.

Though some neo-illiberal voters may support socialist policies, many others do not. The class basis of neo-illiberal voters is usually that of the middle and lower middle classes. The poor, who receive welfare, and ethnic and other minorities, continue to tend to vote for the left, together with upper-middle-class voters. Neo-illiberal voters tend to resent the upper middle class and admire the really rich, or apparently really rich, plutocrats. Therefore, the attempt by some on the left to interpret populist neo-illiberalism as some kind of confused socialism advocated by socialists who do not realize their true calling needs to explain away too much of the evidence.

3

All the Roads Lead to Caesarea

Very fast transitions from apparent liberal democracy to neo-illiberalism indicate that the liberal roots had not sunk deep into the democratic soil before the neo-illiberal whirlwind swept them away. The soil must have been barren or the seeds flew in from faraway lands and could not adjust to the local climate and conditions. The transitions to neo-illiberalism in Venezuela under Chavez, Ecuador under Rafael Correa, and Bolivia under Evo Morales, the smooth dismantling of all the liberal institutions before unfree and unfair "elections" designed to legitimize by popular acclaim the transition to authoritarianism, were too fast and furious for a robust liberal democracy to have ever been there. The liberal institutions were too fragile. Of the countries that had functioning liberal democratic institutions that then gradually eroded to form neo-illiberal democracies, there were two clear and distinct pathways to illiberalism, post-post-totalitarian and post-liberal.

Post-Post-Totalitarian Pathway

European post-totalitarian democracies began their political transitions in 1989 without liberal institutions and civil society (with the possible exceptions of the Catholic Church and Solidarity Trade Union in Poland).

Forty years of totalitarianism atomized civil society and abolished any institutional independence. Pre-totalitarian judicial and other liberal institutions were eviscerated and then maintained as semblances of their former selves for propaganda purposes. They were subsumed under an all-encompassing totalitarian state with a unified single political-social-economic hierarchy that instilled in them subservient norms and habits, appropriate for their low position in the united social hierarchy. The revolutions of 1989 replaced totalitarian with democratically elected governments. But liberal institutions cannot be constructed by elections. They had to be built from scratch in confrontation with norms and interests of bureaucrats who had served totalitarianism, and post-totalitarian elites who wanted private property for themselves without the protections of the rule of law for others. The new political elites that ruled post-Communist countries for the first post-revolutionary twenty years were mostly technocratic, recruited from the professional classes. When populists were elected to replace technocrats, they began fighting the liberalizing institutions, irrespective of the stage of growth and development they had achieved by the time the populists replaced the technocrats.

. The traditional liberal institutions: courts, media, religion, the education system, and so on, existed under totalitarianism, but as empty shells rather than constitutional backbones. They formed departments in the unified state hierarchy, controlled by the Communist Party and its secret police. All the institutions, judges and defense lawyers, priests, journalists, and professors, were receiving instructions from those above them in the unified centralized hierarchy. Democratically elected governments had to confront those institutions, their personnel, and their cultures. At the same time, despite the revolutionary carnivals, civil society was in tatters, with not much between families and the state, after forty years of centralized manipulation of envy and distrust between fellow citizens. The immediate result was an illiberal democracy with institutions and civil servants not so much enforcing the rule of law, to limit the power of the state, as subverting the rule of law, to promote and protect their own interests and those of their erstwhile comrades of the late-totalitarian elite, colloquially known as the nomenklatura. (Formally the nomenklatura meant people whose appointments had to be approved by the Central Committee of the Communist Party.) Their successful common project was the transmutation of political capital into economic capital, while preserving social capital. The old elite did not experience downward mobility, but a lateral social movement, where they transmuted political into economic capital. Society remained passive and atomized into families for decades (Tucker 2015).

Survival in a totalitarian society does not select for emotional expressiveness, especially of political passions. To the extent that the expression of political passions such as revolutionary zeal was coerced, it generated detached irony if not sarcasm. After totalitarianism, survivors preferred to stay at home and attend to their families and gardens. Populism had nothing to offer to them. Elected governments were often of technocrats, especially economists, tasked with fixing the economy and making the people rich like in Germany. When I was teaching in Palacky University in the Czech Republic in the mid-1990s, one of my colleagues began the year by telling the students: "Welcome to Introduction to Economics, or as I call it: How to Become a Millionaire."

The illiberality of technocratic democracy had two opposite effects: On the macro-economic level, post-totalitarian governments could do what democratic governments with active civil society could not, rationalize the economy while ignoring short-term pains and dislocations. The technocrats presented a simple free-market eschatology: short-term economic suffering to expiate for the sins of central planning and nationalization of private property, in return for eternal life in a German-like Eden at the heart of unified Europe. On the micro-economic level, in the absence of rule of law and much law enforcement, corruption by the old elite, some civil servants, and some of the new democratically elected politicians, was unconstrained and at time rapacious. They could distribute the spoils of the economy and occasionally quarrel about them without having to worry about the consequences. Without effective rule of law, corruption, the misuse of public resources and positions for private benefit could not be checked. Corruption did not generate a significant political backlash for twenty years. Post-totalitarian economies were expanding fast and most of the boats seemed to rise in the tide, while the bright European future continued to beacon as manifest destiny. Consequently, when the global recession hit, the macroeconomic state of post-totalitarian states was robust, with little external debt in newly oriented towards export economies. Yet, the already corrupt elites closed themselves and ended mobility. Elite corruption and unjust distribution of scarce resources that had not concerned voters while the economy was expanding, suddenly became noticeable. When at the same time the lights of the shining cities on the Western hills dimmed and ceased to beacon, the moment of neo-illiberal populism arrived.

By twenty years after the end of totalitarianism, when the global recession hit, the liberal institutions of post-Communist countries were in considerably better shape than in 1989. Slow generational personnel replacement brought in younger people, who had clean hands and could not have collaborated with totalitarianism. Later, even better, young people, who were not socialized under totalitarianism, replaced older officials, who retired. But the newer judges and civil servants entered from the bureaucratic bottom and were socialized by their elders. Social continuity from the Communist era implied that morally clean young professionals sometimes had parents they loved, with checkered past. Institutions managed then to reproduce some of their pre-liberal culture. Senior employees who were socialized under totalitarianism still maintained their positions, in the judiciary, the government bureaucracy, the education system, and so on. The *Economist Magazine*, usually a sound judge of quantitative data, had this to say about Poland's judiciary: "The Polish government ... claims that Poland's judiciary was never properly decommunised. This is bunk. The average judge was a teenager when Polish Communism collapsed in 1989" (*Economist*, January 25, 2020, 12). But a bureaucratic hierarchy is not made up of averages, but of seniors and juniors. The senior judges who promote those below them create the institutional culture. Those in their sixties in 2020 were in their thirties in 1989. The late totalitarian elite had its own class interests in mutual solidarity and illicit exchanges with other members of the late-totalitarian elite.

Though the judiciary and the institutions of judicial review were constitutionally constructed liberally as very strong, to check the power of the state they initially misused these powers to slow down the construction of liberal institutions and to protect the interests of the late totalitarian elite, thereby discrediting the courts as politicized and hostile to liberal reforms and the interests of "the people." Ginsburg and Huq (2018, 98) noted the effectiveness of the Hungarian Constitutional Court in striking down a third of the laws between 1990 and 1995. But they did not consider that these were often attempts by Communist judges to block the transition of Hungary from totalitarianism to liberal democracy by blocking the privatization, restitution, and lustration laws, designed both to deal with the past and to open up the elites by excluding former members of the secret police from holding high positions in the government hierarchy.

Since the totalitarian hierarchy had an onion shape, with the Communist Party shadowing institutions and the secret police apparatus controlling the institutions and passing on information to the party, significant number of members of the elite were at least part-time employees or informers of the secret police. Excluding them would have

facilitated liberalization by excluding morally compromised people, while vacating elite positions for new people
who were not part of the Communist establishment. The
judiciary, however, avoided enforcing these laws, either by
excluding the evidence for collaboration as inadmissible,
or by refusing to adjudicate in such cases. In Poland, the
government could not find enough judges to agree to serve
on a lustration court that would have reviewed lustrations,
and so forced the Warsaw District Court to act as one
(Tucker 2015, 60–132). Consequently, the political revolutions of 1989 did not develop into social revolutions. As
long as the economy grew vigorously and the institutions
improved slowly, civil society remained passive.

The economic recessions of the 1990s that followed
the economic transitions and the restructurings of industries were predicted by the technocrats who initiated
them. Politically, those early recessions brought about
the return to power of reformed Communist Parties,
which was known at the time as the "Adamcus effect"
after Lithuania's former-Communist prime minister. But
the reformed technocratic-managerial Communists did
not reverse or even change the course of economic liberalization, and continued the course of economic reforms
that started before their resumption of power, of course
with a good deal of new corruption that lined their own
pockets, as one would expect from good comrades who
were Communists in the 1970s and 1980s. But the second
recession after 2008 came too hard on the heels of the
previous ones, and was not expected. It did not belong to
any meaningful narrative. Heaven should have no recessions, just as it should have no toilets. Post-Communist
societies were not ready for this non-eschatological
meaningless recession. Then, and only then, they started
paying attention to the composition and nature of their
mobility blocking elites.

The neo-illiberal populists appeared then to be the most
credible anti-elite warriors. Whatever else Hungarians
and Poles could accuse Orbán and Kaczyński of, they

could not be accused of collaboration with Communism because they generated and maintained the most extreme anti-Communist public profiles in politics. This street credibility, as the most extreme anti-Communist, more anti-Communist than centrist former dissidents, allowed them to lead populist illiberal revolts against the elites and the liberal institutions that still retained some post-Communist officials. The Czech Republic does not fit this pattern. It had more lustration than Poland and Hungary, since it was the only post-Communist country never to reelect the Communist Party in any reformed shape or form. The Czech mild populists could be led then by a billionaire who was probably a minor Communist secret police collaborator in his youth when he worked in foreign trade in his native Slovakia – such at least nominal collaboration was expected of anybody who dealt with the outside world in a paranoid regime. Prime minister Babiš marketed himself, nevertheless, as a credible anti-elitist and effectively distanced himself from the Communists and their elites (Tucker 2017).

Path Dependency II

From the perspective of political scientists and theorists who studied what was known as "transitions to democracy" in post-totalitarian and post-authoritarian societies (*transitology* for short), the emergence of American and Western European populist neo-illiberal democrats and democracies is ironic. While technocratic liberal democracy appeared the manifest destiny of history, studying Western European politics seemed a shortcut for studying the futures of East European societies. Specialists in West European politics did not need to bother with the intricacies of East European politics, since by the time they finish studying, they would already be West European. Everywhere will become "like Belgium." Now, political theorists of post-Communism may find themselves participating in something like the ironic march in the third movement of Gustav Mahler's First Symphony, which should accompany a funeral procession of forest animals who bury the human hunter. The procession of political scientists who studied authoritarian and totalitarian regimes and their aftermaths, who apply now what they have learned to understand contemporary American and European politics, is similarly ironic. During the 1990s and even during the first decade of the twenty-first century, "transition" experts, *transitologists,* assumed the destiny of the historical process, a convergence with West European and North American technocratic liberal democracy. Now, there is a convergence all right, but of a different kind! Analysis of American and some Western European populist illiberal politics requires comparison with the more advanced stages of populist neo-illiberal democracy in post-totalitarian countries. Viktor Orbán, with a good deal of *chutzpah,* claimed that contemporary Hungary has become the future for Europe rather than the other way around. Viktor Orbán is a "Huey Long" who thinks he is a "Francis Fukuyama."

Sad ironies apart, the path dependencies to illiberal democracy are entirely different. Post-liberal populist movements and governments in countries that were not totalitarian do not owe their popularity to resentment against the persistence of totalitarian elites and hierarchies. This kind of elite does not exist in post-liberal countries. Western liberal institutions are considerably stronger, historically well-entrenched and constitutionally designed to constrain would-be dictators. Their employees and hierarchies have been serving liberal values for generations.

Still, the rise of America's populist illiberal presidency has proved that American politics are not as exceptional as some have wishfully believed: "If, twenty-five years ago, someone had described to you a country in which candidates threatened to lock up their rivals, political opponents accused the government of stealing the election

or establishing a dictatorship, and parties used their legislative majorities to impeach presidents and steal supreme
court seats, you might have thought of Ecuador or
Romania. You probably would not have thought of the
United States" (Levitsky and Ziblatt 2018, 167). Levitsky
and Ziblatt compared Trump's conduct during his first
year in office with other democratically elected illiberals,
according to three sporting metaphoric criteria "capturing
referees," "sidelining competitive players," and "changing
the rules." Trump has attacked the "guardrails," "the
referees," the checks and balances on presidential powers:
law enforcement agencies, intelligence agencies, the
media, the judiciary, and local and state government.
He wanted to use the intelligence agencies to serve him
personally and fired Comey from the FBI, Preet Bharara
from the US attorney office in Manhattan, and Attorney
General Sessions, fired or removed from their positions
the witnesses who testified against him in his impeachment
trial, and submitted the Department of Justice to his will
in the sentencing of his ally Roger Stone, while attacking
the judge and jury. Trump wanted to change libel laws and
misuse licensing and anti-trust laws to muzzle the media.

But, unlike in countries that fall short of the American
constitutional order, the libel laws could not be changed,
nor have the filibuster rules. The Advisory Commission
on Election Integrity (a.k.a voter suppression committee)
was disbanded. Each time the president failed to destabilize established liberal laws or institutions, his critics
breathed a sigh of relief and concluded that the president's
authoritarian threatening bark was worse than his constitutional bite. "President Trump repeatedly scraped up
against the guardrails, like a reckless driver, but he did not
break through them ..." (Levitsky and Ziblatt 2018, 187).
But then the illiberal roller coaster performed another
loop. Trump has proven himself resilient and tireless in
his "marching through the institutions." When he failed
to subvert one institution, he moved on to the next, by
now taking over much of the Justice Department, using

it against law enforcement agencies and the courts, and even attempting to use foreign intelligence services against political competitors and his own intelligence services.

In comparison with Hungary, American decentralization, more than institutional resilience, delayed the neo-illiberal deconstruction. The federal government does not have the kind of powers that states have in centralized small nation-states. Since there was no state-owned media to begin with, Trump could not take it over. In a large media market, though weakened by the internet, media outlets are still financially independent. Government contracts and subsidies are a far smaller share of the economy than in countries like Hungary. Though there is more than enough for personal corruption, government contracts and spending on items like advertising are not as politically useful tools for extensive control over the media and the business sector. Amazon can afford to lose a government contract for cloud services, and whether or not Jeff Bezos will continue to be the richest person in the world depends more on his divorce settlement than on the good graces of Trump. Gerrymandering can take place only on a state level. Some of the judiciary is also locally elected. Much depends not only on the institutions but on the people who operate them – whether they are opportunistic, and if so, how do they predict future political trends? Trump found it challenging to find people able and willing to assume the mantle of neo-illiberal bureaucratic warriors outside the Republican Party.

Americans have been socialized into believing in a liberal free market system with functioning institutions, where private vices like greed and lust for power are routinely transmuted into public virtues. They are used to pursuing their private interests with abandon and ignoring their public effects because they usually turn out right, or at least not criminal. But when the institutions themselves are infected with corruption, or become dysfunctional, vices remain vices on all levels. In the absence of historical experience of occupation and local collaboration, Americans find it hard to imagine that private vices can remain vices all the way up. The obvious example is the incredibly quick and complete transition of the Republican Party and republican oriented elites from ideologically liberal-conservatives to neo-illiberal populists, because Trump won and gained the power to distribute jobs, privileges, and funding. This is of course an alliance of convenience rather than conviction. But radical opportunists do not see the difference. The same would happen to other elites should they believe that Trump has gained control over more than a diminishing Republican Party, and the American nation has turned illiberal populist for a generation. No poll has indicated such a radical transition, and the elections of 2018 indicate otherwise. For now, prudent non-republicans would not gamble with their careers over the results of the 2020 elections.

The republican elite's opportunistic conversion to populist neo-illiberalism demonstrates the weakness of institutions when their elites defect. Their rationalizations of collaboration are hackneyed: If they do not do it, somebody worse will, they may be in a position to prevent the worst of it, they will be able to influence more from the inside, and so on. They did not "follow orders," but did a job for which they were paid well. There are roads from opportunism to betrayal that have been paved and repaved with excuses many times in history – just ask Alcibiades.

A decade ago, Signer (2009) published a book about demagogues and democracy. He argued that the rise of demagogues is a symptom of deeper problems that make people willingly enslave themselves. His polemical purpose in the context of the George W. Bush presidency and the war in Iraq was to debate the democratic fundamentalism of the "neocons" who considered the spread of democracy the panacea for all political evils, while ignoring the historical, social, and institutional contexts where democracy has been successful and, more importantly, those where it was not. Rather than argue that liberal institutions are necessary conditions for democracy that does not destroy itself, and conclude that liberal institutions must be in place or quickly develop before democracy can be successfully transplanted, Signer argued that Jeffersonian constitutional values, the correct people rather than their institutions, were missing in places like Iraq and Palestinian Gaza. The citizens of the United States, rather than their institutions, held American democracy together, despite temporary bouts of populism and elite failures. Signer believed that a *culture* of American constitutionalism is the primary check on authoritarianism in America.

By the supreme ironic powers of the gods of history ("Man plans, God laughs"), in 2016 Signer was elected mayor of Charlottesville in Virginia, the university town that Thomas Jefferson founded near his home in Monticello. In the summer of 2017, it was the site of the "Unite the Right" rally of American neo-Nazis that resulted in the murder of a liberal protester and the injury of others. President Trump commented that "there were good people on both sides." One can only divine that the conclusion Clio, the goddess of history, tries to teach us is that "it can happen anywhere!" Constitutional values are not entrenched even in the oldest continuously existing large liberal constitutional democracy, and their absence can be manifested at the very shrine of Jeffersonian democracy. Liberal culture and institutions must all work together.

It looks as though the liberal values that were attributed to NATO countries during the Cold War were not as deeply entrenched as they seemed. Liberal democracy must fall back, then, on constitutional design. The most obvious example is Italy's proportional representation election system, designed to prevent concentration of power. Italy was fortunate that prime minister Renzi's reckless plebiscite to change that system failed. Italian governments are unstable, but that also means that a neo-illiberal takeover is more difficult, as the populist illiberal demagogue Mateo Salvini discovered when he found himself out of government. To return to power, he will have to form another coalition that again would be unstable. This attests to the wisdom of the framers of the 1947 Italian Constitution who traded stability for liberty.

A House Divided: Prognostic Instability

Illiberal democracy, old and new, is unstable. The old, classical, illiberal democracy was unstable because, sooner or later, the democratic state and society came under extreme existential stress, military defeats, economic crises, social conflicts between factions and classes, or diseases and plagues. When reason failed to resolve these crises, the passions flared and led to the self-destruction of democracy and the rise of authoritarianism. Illiberal democratic regimes cared only for their popularity with the majority or substantial minority of the population that supported them, their base. Minorities and other outsiders did not count. This led to instability because the minority losers would fight back if they could, or even ally with foreign enemies of the majority.

Contemporary neo-illiberal democracies are embarking on a very old road from democracy to authoritarianism, a road trodden by numerous democracies in the ancient and modern world. Liberalism and its institutions are in the way, blocking this ancient road. To become tyrants in the ancient mold, the modern neo-illiberal demagogues must first dismantle the liberal institutional barriers to absolutism, fragment civil society, and then fix the results of elections. Neo-illiberal regimes are in relentless, asymmetrical, war of attrition against the liberal institutions that should check their powers. The battle fronts are unstable, shifty, and dynamic. The constant scraping against the liberal guardrails turns quickly into shoving matches where one side or the other must give way. This is the cause of much of the "drama" that accompanies illiberal democracy. The political system can be stabilized, either when neo-illiberal democracy transitions into authoritarianism, or when it reverts to liberal democracy by strong institutions and disillusioned voters. I argue that there is no stable equilibrium that is neither liberal nor authoritarian. Levitsky and Ziblatt distinguished three possible scenarios for neo-illiberal democracy: *hybrid authoritarianism*, *liberal restoration*, and *continued illiberal democracy*. I argue that only the first two are likely.

Budapest on the Potomac

Levitsky and Ziblatt (2018, 5) highlighted, using metaphors from competitive team sports, the three mutually reinforcing processes that gradually transform democracies into hybrid authoritarian regimes: Illiberal governments come to control the "referees" of the political game, especially the *judiciary*; they weaken their opponents by expelling from the political arena the most competitive "players" for other teams (as Trump attempted to do to Joe Biden); and, finally, they change the rules of the political "game" to ensure that they will continue to win apparently pluralistic and free elections indefinitely, irrespective of the popular vote. The same "bully or bribe" tactics are then applied to politically relevant sectors of civil society, the media, non-governmental organizations, and wealthy, powerful, or otherwise influential individuals. Once illiberal governments manage to rewrite constitutions, control their judicial interpretations and electoral systems, they can prolong their tenure indefinitely, and neo-illiberal democracy becomes absolutist and authoritarian. This process takes time. Elected leaders, legislatures, and the courts must work together to dismantle checks and balances, pack the courts, buy or intimidate the media, and harass political opponents. There is no single revolutionary event, no storming of the Bastille or the Winter Palace, and no burning Reichstag.

Levitsky and Ziblatt did not exclude a "burning Reichstag" scenario, the manipulation of a security crisis to silence the opposition, rally public opinion, and facilitate an authoritarian takeover, but found it unlikely. Still, such a crisis happened unexpectedly, like on 9/11, but it was not a security crisis as many predicted, but a health catastrophe that generated an economic collapse. Blundering amateur political ignorance and inexperience exacerbated further what would have been a serious shock to any regime, liberal technocracy or illiberal democracy. The medical emergency of the coronavirus plague was the kind of surprising unpredictable "burning Reichstag" that neo-illiberals could seize on to assume absolute power, as in Hungary. Other neo-illiberals will attempt to follow in Orbán's footsteps, starting in Poland and Israel. There is an odd parallel here between the death of democracy and death from Covid-19. Those who suffer from "preexisting conditions," medical or political, respectively, have a much higher chance of dying from it. Neo-illiberal democracies that had the weakest liberal institutions, also have had the highest chance of turning into authoritarian regimes following the pandemic existential and economic crisis. Healthier liberal democracies are less likely to turn authoritarian, even when, like post-authoritarian Spain, they suffer higher rates of disease and death than less liberal countries.

Ginsburg and Huq (2018) agreed it is cheaper for autocrats to slowly but relentlessly and insidiously curtail liberal institutions and traditions, with no sharp inflection point. They dismantle the rule of law by packing the courts, intimidating judges, and scaring the bureaucracy into submission by firing or harassing bureaucrats till they resign, *pour encourager les autres*, and by rewarding or punishing them through their salaries, promotions, and other working conditions. Once the bureaucracy and judiciary are subdued, the executive unleashes them on political opponents or competitors. Revisions to election rules through gerrymandering techniques eliminate or radically disadvantage the political opposition. For example, after changing the Hungarian Constitution, Fidesz won in 2014 a two-thirds parliamentary majority with 45 percent of the vote. Ginsburg and Huq emphasized that in most authoritarian power grabs legislation was used to undermine legality and then kill democracy by a thousand cuts. There is no need then to rely on the burning Reichstag – the Reichstag can be decommissioned instead, office by office, then wing by wing. Finally, when forgotten, it will be closed down and put for sale; an oligarch will buy it, with the proceeds going for the ruling neo-illiberals.

Regimes that do not enjoy wide popular trust and legitimacy find it difficult to wage wars that are not won quickly and cheaply. For this reason, authoritarian Latin American military regimes were reluctant to wage wars against *foreign* adversaries. When the Argentinian Junta violated this rule, it self-destructed, courtesy of the British military. Napoleon III waged quick and easy colonial and papal wars, but he was careful, for almost two decades, not to follow his step-uncle's adventures. Once he did, the result was Sedan and the ultimate democratic restoration in France that has lasted now for 150 years, courtesy of the Prussian Army. Similarly, at least in Israeli terms, Netanyahu has been exceptionally cautious in his use of the military. He attacked the weak Palestinians in Gaza, but has been careful to attack Iran only clandestinely and verbally. The neo-illiberal leaders who ride populist waves, like their ancient illiberal colleagues, manipulate populist passions, but are careful not to channel them into significant external aggression. The self-destruction of neo-illiberalism is unlikely to come from foreign adventures, though surprises are possible if illiberal leaders cannot contain the passions, fall into the trap of their own rhetoric, or if they stumble into war unintentionally, by miscalculation.

The gradual deconstruction of liberal institutions may result in gerrymandered permanent illiberal electoral majorities, voter suppression, and a subservient judicial system, which Orbán has achieved in Hungary over a decade of relentless efforts. Levitsky and Ziblatt consider such a scenario unlikely, though conceivable, for the United States. Eric Posner (2018) also found an American "transition to authoritarianism," implausible. Trump would have to take over Congress. "Some dictators prevail over the legislature because they are immensely popular and call on the public to punish legislative opponents in the polls" (Posner 2018, 6). Trump has achieved this total control over his party, but lost control over the House of Representatives in the process.

Posner emphasized the interdependence between the institutions that check and balance the power of the presidency. They cannot work well without mutual support. For example, the judiciary cannot check the executive without enforcement by the bureaucracy and protection by the legislature of its independence. Posner noted that over time, many small steps may breach the defenses against dictatorship. Trump has been attacking verbally and attempting to bully the courts and the Justice Department, until he appointed an Attorney General who obeys. The appointment of attorney general Barr, a genuine illiberal absolutist, started a process that should submit the Justice Department to Trump's whims. As Ginsburg and Huq put it: "Although as a matter of tradition, Justice Department lawyers have maintained a sense of fidelity to the law over political direction, there is no structural reason that this norm could not be undermined through the appointment of an aggressively partisan attorney general with personal loyalty to the president. Indeed, to the extent that a president runs as a charismatic populist and rails against existing elites, we think it is quite possible for him to target overtly the conventions of Justice Department integrity, and to make the politicizing capture of that department a central plank of his political agenda" (Ginsburg and Huq 2018, 229). This is exactly what has been happening recently. Trump and the Netanyahu government have also been appointing many judges, though unlike in Hungary and Poland, they have not been able to fire or retire judges.

Control of the bureaucracy also grows slowly and incrementally. True, "Trump is hampered by the small number of truly loyal supporters who also have significant government experience and hence the ability to control the agencies they are asked to head" (Posner 2018, 8). But this is true only in the short term. Over time, alternative elites, loyal to the Trump dynasty, have been emerging. Careerists and opportunists in the pre-Trump elites, in and out of the bureaucracy, act on the shared belief that the Trump episode may well be temporary, and will be followed by a restoration that has already begun with the Democratic victory in the 2018 congressional elections. If so, those who fly too close to the sunny-faced president will burn and crash once he loses the elections, if not earlier, since Trump is not a loyal patron. If this common assessment is revised, if Trump wins again in 2020, opportunist elites and bureaucrats will join the Republicans in fearing and loathing their president in private, while obeying and supporting him in public, and authoritarian illiberalism will be entrenched.

Posner emphasized that even had Trump controlled the federal bureaucracy, illiberals would still need to work through state and local layers of government. Still, neo-illiberal democrats may gain local control by reapplying the toolkit of dirty tricks they use on the national level on local levels. Ginsburg and Huq (2018) noted that some of the hallmark policies of illiberal regimes such as Orbán's have already been tried on local levels in the United States: Wisconsin republicans won 60 percent of the seats with less than a plurality of the votes, and North Carolina's republican legislators attempted to strip the powers of their governor once a Democrat was elected. However, local democracy can overcome the neo-illiberal uneven playing field and generate liberal victories, even in the mature neo-illiberal post-democracies of Hungary and Poland, in the major urban centers that are mostly liberal. In Poland, the opposition also won the recent 2019 Senate elections.

American civil society seems vibrant. Posner identified civil society with still independent professionals, lawyers, scientists, and academics. But, with the help of Congress, Trump has demonstrated the social weakness of scientists and academics by ignoring their advice, and by imposing a low tax on university endowments, and income tax on tuition remissions to students, intimidating shots across the bow of academia. Neo-illiberals do not need to disband or take over societies of experts. They are not totalitarian. They can just ignore them or, even better, use them as scapegoats for popular resentment. The coronavirus crisis will challenge this approach as the neo-illiberals need the experts both to avert total disaster and to scapegoat for the inevitable costs. But logical internal contradictions can co-exist in populist passionate political narratives.

Ginsburg and Huq (2018, 120–163) argued that the US Constitution cannot defend liberal rights from neo-illiberal democrats because it can be interpreted as upholding the absolute powers of executive government, to expand and incrementally erode and eviscerate the liberal institutions that should check its power. "The US Constitution may be good at checking coups or the antidemocratic deployment of emergency powers, but it is not well suited to stall the slow decay of democracy" (151). The American traditions of voter suppression and the transmutation of temporary to permanent majorities proves it. A constitution cannot be much more effective than those who interpret and enforce it. "Democracy demands from its participants a certain political morality. In the absence of that political morality, nothing in the toolkit of constitutional designers will save constitutional democracy. Design ... can go only so far without decency" (Ginsburg and Huq 2018, 173). As the post-Habsburg states proved, liberal democracy cannot survive long in the absence of liberal democrats, even when the constitutions are imported from the best sources. The political and social legacies of the constitution can slow down, delay, and impose costs on democratic backsliding. But they cannot hold it off indefinitely. A constitution cannot protect, preserve, and defend a republic with too few republicans. The question for the third decade of the twenty-first century will be: How many liberal democrats are left there after the biological, economic, social, and political shocks that rocked traditional and new liberal democracies in quick succession, in this, thus-far, anxious century?

The Surf Beaches of Utopia

For better or worse, California could be the future of humanity. Trump could lose the 2020 elections decisively. The political carnival with its jester king would come to a sobering end, with a huge medical hangover from the pandemic and the size of the national debt. As though with PG13 (parental guidance), political life would stabilize on the basis of a new liberal consensus. Trump's defeat will reverberate throughout the world. Liberalism will regain its soft and geopolitical powers, as well as its confidence, its "mojo." Populism will lose its fashionable edge and will become outdated and boring, associated with cranky old losers. The world will move on with economic vibrancy and technological innovation to new sunny uplands of civilization.

California had suffered from ethnic and cultural wars for over a generation until an overwhelming multi-cultural and multi-ethnic liberal absolute majority founded on prosperity and high technology has emerged. Orange County, traditionally the bastion of American Conservatism, has now a Democratic Party majority. Illiberals and other anti-Californians, on Fox News for example, like to highlight the problems California, or at least its urban tech hubs, suffer from: high costs of living – especially housing, homelessness, and inequality. These problems, like immigration, are actually indicators of economic success. The homeless prefer to live on wealthy streets rather than in cheaper rural America.

Levitsky and Ziblatt (2018) considered this California style liberal restoration scenario unlikely because of the long-term polarizing trends in the United States that long preceded Trump. Norris and Inglehart (2019) and other progressives (Pinker 2018) have taken the opposite position. They argue that long-term demographic trends, growing ethnic and cultural diversity in the United States, gradual enlightenment, increasingly liberal and tolerant younger generations, increasing scientific knowledge and economic prosperity, decreasing passions, especially the ones that lead to violence, all point toward the "California-zation" of the world, or at least the United States. Current illiberal democracy may be a bump on the progressive road to the surf beaches of utopia. Political appearances to the contrary, Pinker (2018) alluded to deep social and economic progressive trends that affect the lives of most people more than the results of elections. Politics may simply not be as important as it may seem, seafoam above the progressive deep current. Those liberalizing currents will eventually sink the populist illiberal ship of state and have it join the wreckages of other doomed lost causes from the Confederacy to Communism.

Norris and Inglehart (2019) went further, to claim that the electoral victories of illiberal populists are desperate reactions to a demographic inflection point, when young multi-ethnic liberals demographically overwhelm their reactionary elders. Just before they are swept off the face of history, the forces of reaction stage a last stand and appoint ancient clowns as their generals. Norris and Inglehart acknowledged a little problem for this narrative: The young liberal progressives do not go to vote to the extent that their ancient opponents do and so do not affect the results of elections. As Mounk (2018) noted, this alienation from the democratic political process and the democratic institutions are long-term trends that push in the opposite direction. Further, young Northern Europeans (and some Israelis), who vote for neo-illiberal populists, share the prevailing liberal values that Norris and Inglehart cited as indicators of progress; for example, they support LGBT rights and protecting the environment.

Dynamic Equilibria

I do not want to speculate here on which of the two sets of trends will overwhelm the other, and when or where it will happen, though it is as difficult to imagine a liberal Hungary as surfers on the Danube or Budapest on the pacific coast in the foreseeable future. I do argue, though, that liberalism and authoritarianism, "California" and "Hungary," can be stable. California liberalism survived the recession and is even stronger than before; it even seems relatively effective in mitigating the effects of the coronavirus in terms of dead and infected per capita in comparison with other populous urban American states. It is difficult to imagine a coalition of forces that would unseat Orbán in Hungary without significant foreign assistance from the European Union and its member states. The urban middle classes and their liberal institutions are missing outside the only urban center, Budapest.

But there is no stable political space between California and Hungary. Neo-illiberal democracy is highly unstable. Levitsky and Ziblatt (2018) held the opposite view, thinking that the most likely prognostic scenario, at least for the United States, would resemble the politics of North Carolina. The guardrails of democracy will weaken in the context of increased polarization and political and cultural strife, gerrymandering, and surgical suppression of minority votes. The battle lines between democracy and liberalism would remain unstable in a constant war of attrition. In my opinion, neo-illiberal democracy is inherently unstable because of the constant struggle between the government and the institutions. This struggle can end only with the victory of one side. The instability in the middle favors the stable extremes. Once the system touches one extreme, it stabilizes and stays there.

Another kind of stability may be cyclical: Since populism, by definition, is self-destructive, to the extent that neo-illiberal populists in power take their own rhetoric literally and seriously, or are forced to act on their promises, they initiate their own political self-destruction. For example, populist economic policies that privilege immediate gratification over long-term growth often require heavy state borrowing to create unsustainable temporary prosperity and, consequently, a debt crisis, pressure on the currency, and inflation, the classical cycle of Latin American populism. Populist xenophobic policies limit trade and immigration at the cost of lower competitiveness and growth, higher inflation, and greater pressure on the younger generation to pay for transfer payments to their elders, the classical economic mistakes of the 1930s and of Japan today.

Sufficiently destructive policies eventually cause the economy to keel over, collapse under the accumulated weight of deficits, debts, or inflation, and unemployment that results from the collapse of international trade. This collapse can push the country over to authoritarianism. The authoritarians may stabilize the economy by bringing in technocrats, while suppressing social discontent. Eventually, the authoritarian rulers, perhaps under international or internal pressure, or following tensions within the authoritarian regime, may initiate political liberalization. Illiberal or weakly liberal democracy may then return, until it comes under pressure, which results in populism and so on and so forth. Such cycles were typical of Latin American politics. Stability then may not be of a regime type, but of a cycle of regimes. Adam Przeworski (1991, 1995) forecast after the fall of Communism that post-Communist democracies would resemble Latin American democracies, locked in a cycle where authoritarianism and populist democracy replace each other. For twenty years this theory seemed totally wrong. Post-Communist societies and polities did not develop mass populist movements, but were content with democratic technocracies that were developing in a mildly liberal direction. But his prediction may now come true.

Populist self-destruction can be militaristic, as in Ancient Athens, or in Louis Napoleon's war with Germany, or it can be economic, through policies that destroy the economy. So far, the neo-illiberals in power have been prudent enough to avoid the kind of military conflicts that may inflict sufficient damage on the populist perpetrator to trigger a collapse. Trump's reputation for instability and impulsivity may also have deterred potential aggressors. The prospects for economic self-destruction are far more promising.

Economic populism is at the intersections of two cycles, the economic boom-bust cycle, and the populist political cycle that follows it. These two cycles are not simultaneous. When the populist cycle starts, when the recovery stage from the economic bust is under way, policies that would have been considered populist during the bust, are just profligate or generous during recovery, when tax revenues can cover them. For example, the populists in East Europe "bought" constituencies with public funds. The Polish government instituted generous child benefits, while the Czech populists increased the salaries of teachers by 15 percent. High economic growth followed the economic dividends from East Europe's integration into the European Union and, especially in the German economy, the increased exports of manufactured goods and workers. But the debt that finances Trump's tax deductions may justify the populist label and fit a cyclical model. The accumulation of debt cannot go on indefinitely, and the relatively independent economic cycle may be postponed, but not abolished. When the economy goes into a recession again, the accumulated debt and low taxes would make counter-cyclical moves more difficult, deepen such a recession, and initiate a political counter-populist cycle that does not have to be liberal or democratic, but must be technocratic. This will, however, take time. The economic cycle is not aligned well with the political cycle.

But it may be happening about now, following global coronavirus recessions.

Though there are no stable neo-illiberal democracies, I hesitate to make further predictions about eventual political equilibria in each country, authoritarian, liberal, or cyclical. The main reason for refraining from predictions is that the apparent current wave of illiberalism is not a wave at all, but a series of unfortunate events that were not inevitable. Many small contingencies coincided to bring about an apparent wave that otherwise could have remained under the political surface, as I show next.

4

It Ain't Necessarily So: The Historical Evitability of Neo-Illiberal Democracy

In the second decade of the twenty-first century, democrats and liberals watched helplessly as recession gave way to slow growth, and rising inequality undermined social comity and trust in the mythical progressive shining light at the end of the long tunnel of history. As the economic crisis spilled over from Manhattan's financial district to gradually cover the whole world, the putrid concoction of economic stagnation and unemployment cracked the upper crust of the postwar liberal world order. The cracked crust allowed a witch's brew of political passions to boil to the surface. Floating on the putrid mixture, from the bottom of the political barrel, vulgar and vile populist neo-illiberal politicians propelled themselves to form a new crust. Historically conscious observers sensed overwhelming noxiousness, as though suffering from food poisoning again from a similar dish. A self-inflicted sense of helplessness can be expressed metaphysically as a belief in historical inevitability, just as a noxious sense of historical *déjà-vu* fits a cyclical concept of history, at least of the past two centuries.

Historical inevitability and economic determinism are back in vogue, for the first time since the aftermath of the Great Depression, when they matched the fashionable Marxist ideology of the time. They can explain the apparent divide between open and closed societies, between norms of embracing tolerance, innovation, plurality, and diversity, and those that would arrest change to restore an imaginary past to shelter fragile, insecure identities by differences as small as between national two percent (the post-2009 average rate in the United States) and four percent GDP growth (in much of the 1990s) per annum, averaged over a decade. When the differences are larger, as between the negative growth of the 1930s and the high growth of the 1960s, it is possible to predict the difference between the storm troopers and the hippies, blitzkrieg and the counterculture, Auschwitz and Ashbury.

Another kind of "history is destiny" cultural, rather than economic, determinism would note the similarities between the map of neo-illiberalism and populism in Europe today and the map of authoritarian regimes in Europe in the 1930s (minus North-Western Germany), just as there is similarity between the map of the Confederacy in the American Civil War and the map of states that gave Trump the presidency (minus Virginia, plus Pennsylvania and parts of the Midwest). Perhaps glacially changing political cultures are destiny. Either way, democracy happens only in some places, typically between economic recessions.

Questions in the philosophy of history that dominated the middle of the twentieth century but were then abandoned, rather than resolved, have returned with a vengeance: Is history evitable or inevitable? What is the role of the individual, or "hero," in history? Is history cyclical, progressive, regressive, or directionless? Does history repeat itself, or merely rhyme? Can we learn from history and what is the role of historiography in this process? These questions return with poignant urgency. The philosophical cycle may follow a historical cycle; these questions in the philosophy of history were raised following the consecutive crises of advanced economies in the 1930s, the collapse of democracies, the rise of two particularly virulent types of totalitarianisms, the self-destruction of Europe, and then the Cold War. The totalitarian power that survived and won the Second World War expressed allegiance to a robust philosophy of history, Marxism, thereby pushing philosophers of history to the forefront of the war of ideas that accompanied the Cold War. The liberal democratic ideological victory in the Cold War that preceded the political victory of 1989–1991 by a generation or so, seemed to have made these questions obsolete, but they have returned from the dead, reinvigorated to haunt us.

There have been four, I would say, *attitudes* to these questions, since it would be a stretch to call all of them *philosophies of history*. Unlike totalitarianism, liberalism and progressivism, contemporary populism does not really have a philosophy of history, or even an ideology, because the closest thing it has to an ideology is anti-intellectualism. Populism definitely has an attitude though. These attitudes to the questions of the philosophy of history can be summarized systematically in the table below.

Totalitarian philosophies of history considered history inevitable because they thought large impersonal forces such as race and class determine history. They reduced history to biological or economic caricatures. When totalitarian ideologies began to promote personality cults of revolutionary leaders, they generated an inner contradiction: If history is inevitable, why should Lenin, Stalin, Gottwald, Kim, or Hitler matter? The ideological response resorted to the logical "part–whole fallacy," the identification of the properties of a whole with those of its parts. The totalitarian leaders ceased being individuals and became identified with the historical whole, may it be class or nation. The reduction of the whole to its part proceeds as a series of transitive reductions: History = the people = the class or race = the party = the cadres/ the SS = the leader, hence, history = the leader. The totalitarian concept of history was cyclical. History repeats itself in periodic

Four Ideologies and Philosophies of History

	Totalitarian	Liberal	Progressive	Populist
Historical Inevitability/ Evitability	Inevitable	Evitable	Inevitable	Too many syllables/ pass
History is made by Individuals vs. Impersonal Forces	Large impersonal forces, with cult figures	Individualist	Impersonal processes	Individualist
Direction of History	Cyclical	Conditionally progressive	Absolutely progressive	Regressive
Historical Repetition vs. Uniqueness	Repetitive	Unique	Unique	Repetitive
Can History Teach Lessons for the Present?	No, except for the "laws" of history and few tactical lessons	Yes; learn from mistakes	No; history is always new.	No; boring.

cycles of class or racial conflicts. The aim of totalitarian utopias was to end or transcend history by putting a stop to it, to generate classless or racially pure societies, future utopias that would also mark a return to primeval nature when hunter-gatherers had no private property or when noble savage Siegfrieds fought each other without the encumbrances of conscience. If history is necessary and inevitable, it cannot teach anything relevant for the future. Like the revolutions of the earth around the sun, it will happen whether we understand it or not, because there is nothing we can do about it. If the historical process can be likened to a pregnancy, we can at most "shorten the birth pangs," as Marx put it. At most, the revolutionary vanguard may learn some practical tactical lessons from its historical experience.

Anti-totalitarian liberal noble warriors like Karl Popper and Isaiah Berlin retorted that history is not preordained, but contingent. Minor events can have major consequences. Individual decisions, choices, folly, genius, and virtue, can intentionally or with unforeseen consequences affect the course of history. Liberals perceived historical progressive trends in parts of the world: economic growth since the European Middle Ages, cultural and scientific progress since the Renaissance, and political progress since the Glorious and American Revolutions, if not since Magna Carta. But this progress has been conceived as conditional on historical contexts and circumstances. Liberal progress is not the destiny of humanity. Liberal studies of modernity, democratization, economic progress, and their interconnections have attempted to discover the historical preconditions, the winning formula, or stimulating causes that nudge history in the direction that liberal values designate progressive, increasing freedom, knowing full well that decisions have historical consequences and there is no progressive inevitability. History does not, or at any rate need not, repeat itself. "Some people believe that history repeats itself, others read the *Economist*," as the advertisement for the liberal magazine went.

Though history is not cyclical or repetitive, liberals believed that much could be learned from it, especially from past mistakes and wrong turns. This learning process especially affected the construction of institutions. The founders of the United States studied the self-destruction of the Roman Republic as they set out to build a new republic on better institutional constitutional foundations. At the end of the Second World War liberal policymakers in the West set out to construct a political, social, and global institutional order that would prevent recurrence of the mistakes of the first half of the twentieth century, especially the policy mistakes that led to the transmutation of a financial crisis generated by a few banks into a global calamity that nearly sent the modern world the way of the Roman Empire; the political errors that allowed anti-democratic political parties to take over states with a minority of the votes and the geopolitical missteps that allowed aggressive totalitarian states to build up their militaries, rearm, and start wars against individual states that could not form effective anti-totalitarian alliances, and were ready to sacrifice each other for their national interests. Liberals were all too aware that it could have been otherwise. Wiser decisions and better institutions in the 1930s may have preempted the globalization of the crisis, could have forestalled the rise of totalitarianism, and prevented the Second World War by decisive joint military action; for example after the Nazis entered the Rhineland, a point Churchill made to the American Congress in his speech there after the United States finally joined the Second World War, in which Churchill foresaw the overwhelming reasons to found NATO after the war. These institutional reforms created the basis for the world order that is now disintegrating.

Progressives believe in *inevitable* historical progress. They believe history has a direction and that the purpose of history is positive. History then progresses toward this end, irrespective of what people in history intend, think or feel. This view of history emerged with the Enlightenment and reached its zenith in the long nineteenth century. It has strong theological foundations as a secularized Judeo-Christianity. The world-wide senseless slaughter of the First World War, the rise of totalitarianism, genocide in the Second World War, and the atom bomb, seemed to have cruelly killed off the progressive philosophy of history. It gained a second life in the United States since the 1960s as civil rights movements advocating for women, racial, ethnic and sexual minorities progressed and expanded freedom and equality in a process that appeared linear and gradual, yet incredibly rapid from a historical perspective. Progressive philosophy of history received a further boost from the implosion of totalitarian and authoritarian regimes in the last quarter of the twentieth century, the apparent third wave of the end of history.

As President Obama put it, quoting Martin Luther King (who was not the first to use the expression) "the arc of the moral universe is long, but it bends toward justice." Philosophers like Peter Railton (1986) formulated this approach as a version of "moral realism" that believes history progresses through the competition between societies that leads to survival of morally fit societies. Railton and other moral realists believe in an evolutionary selection process that gives evolutionary advantage to liberal moral societies that respect the rights of subgroups and minorities. Much as nature gave an advantage to giraffes with increasingly long necks, the social evolutionary process favors liberal societies, and thereby makes them necessary. Irrespective of the natural variation and different base states of societies in history, the successful liberal models will necessarily tend to survive and reproduce. Since progressive change is eventually inevitable, despite historical twists and turns, the teleological arc of history does *not* usually repeat itself, as it bends toward justice. For example, Steven Pinker's (2012) *Better Angels of our Nature* will continue to lead humanity away from its violent barbarian past to a pacifist progressive future unconditionally and spontaneously without necessary human intentional agency or vigilance or other historical conditions. Progressive individuals can join the great march to justice, but they do not have to. The march will reach its goal anyway.

Accordingly, studying history and the philosophy of history became redundant for the construction of a progressive world founded on technological advancements, increasing prosperity, and growing egalitarianism based on empathy. Scientific managers and engineers would solve the problems that baffled philosophers, historians, and social thinkers by generating progress. Managers and other technocrats should not be bound by historical lessons; they should not stick to what worked in the past – that is conservatism, and should not be deterred from trying new ideas even if they are old ideas that may have failed in the past, because progressive history does not repeat itself. Central planning in 2020 may not be like central planning in 1920 (a liberal could agree to the extent that some big data mining could preempt some central planning mistakes; but otherwise, to paraphrase Beckett it would be a case of fail again, fail better). The contingency that civilization might have to fall back on its historical lessons when the technocratic managerial locomotive of progress jumps the track did not appear realistic. The economic track jump of 2007–2009 and the political track jump of 2016–2017 (and one may add the health track jump of 2020, the return of a pandemic after a century), taken together, mark "Santayana's revenge," the return of history to haunt those who denied it. No, professor Pangloss, we do not live in the best of all possible worlds. Scientific and technological progress did not preempt the deepest recession since the thirties, the rise of neo-illiberalism, or the return of a pandemic of the kind that was common until the Spanish flu a century ago.

Norris and Inglehart (2019) reiterated the classical case for progressivism a decade after the economic crisis, three years into Trump's presidency, and months away from the pandemic. As in classical modernization theory, economic progress, urbanization, and education, have led to a progressive decline in authoritarian value systems and rise in liberal values since the Second World War. The youth revolts of the by now retired boomers in the 1960s have boosted this process. Now, we are at the very point of inflexion, before the final victory of modern progressivism and the end of "white" ethnic dominance in the United States, the final end of history. The reactionary, old, rural, and uneducated white males somehow sense viscerally that their time is up and they are about to be swept from history, and so they led a rearguard last stand before their inevitable political and indeed biological demise. Their reactionary struggle is all the more ferocious for its desperate hopelessness. The apparent defeat of progress is the result of the curious tendency of the young, urban, educated, multi-cultural, and multi-ethnic vanguards of progress to stay at home on Election Day, while their reactionary elders show admirable discipline in their voting habits.

Yascha Mounk cited statistical polling data that demonstrate the opposite, gradual decline in the popularity of democracy and rise in the acceptance of authoritarianism across countries in the West that had preceded the economic crisis and the subsequent political crises of the second decade of the twenty-first century. Democracy enjoyed legitimacy as long as it "kept the peace and swelled [the]... notebooks" (Mounk 2018, 131). Democracies suffer now from "performance crisis." Norris and Inglehart and Mounk's diametrically opposed conclusions are based on statistical studies that measured different values as proxies for authoritarian versus democratic or liberal values. The values that Norris' surveys measured were more cultural and less political than the values Mounk's surveys examined. Norris studied conservative values about gender equality, fluidity, and choice. Mounk studied directly attitudes to democracy and its institutions.

Even had Mounk and Norris and Inglehart been able to reconcile the statistical data bases and agree on the axiological trends and their directions, there has been no simple correspondence between values and regimes. Sexual liberation, historically, goes well with authoritarianism. Greek and Roman tyrants and demagogues were sexually "liberal" to say the least. The Nazis had also been quite tolerant of homosexuality, until Hitler found it politically expedient to attack the openly homosexual Ernst Röhm. Contemporary West European and Israeli populist neo-illiberals use their sexual tolerance to "pink wash" their xenophobia against allegedly intolerant migrants, though of course they do not advocate granting asylums to LGBT individuals from Moslem countries. Vice versa, historically, many liberal democrats reflected the patriarchal values of their era. The current association of conservative sexuality with authoritarianism and sexual liberty with liberalism is historically contingent and holds clearly only among fundamentalists, conservative Catholics, and in Poland and Hungary. Netanyahu, by contrast, appointed an openly gay member of his party as Justice Minister in charge of dismantling the rule of law. The liberal democratic compromise was a distant second best for most of the religious fanatics who constructed it in Britain and the United States. Their values surely were neither liberal not democratic, yet their balance of intolerances generated a stable liberal equilibrium. Vice versa, "post-materialist" values taken to the extreme can generate a form of intolerant authoritarianism that persecutes those who happen to dissent or appear to dissent from its orthodox values. The emphasis on measuring popular values as the basis for political regimes is an extreme form of idealism that does not consider that values through institutions can transmute into their opposites. There has never been a simple linear relation between values and politics.

Contemporary populism is entirely ahistorical. It is not just ignorant of the mistakes of the past that it unwittingly attempts to repeat, but it lacks *any* historical orientation in time, any historical consciousness beyond a vaguely reactionary, mostly inarticulate, sense that history has been regressive lately; but that a strong leader may halt the decline and make history young again.

Historical Evitability

Totalitarian and progressive philosophies of history agree about its inevitability. They just disagree about the content of that inevitable course of events. Populists do not reflect about the question of historical evitablity, but their self-unreflective sleepwalking through some of the most disturbing aspects of history fits in practice if not in theory a "mice in a treadmill" concept of the position of humans in history. I want to challenge these attitudes to the philosophy of history and defend a liberal philosophy of history. I argue that the populist neo-illiberal democracies of the second decade of the twenty-first century were largely evitable. Therefore, there is good reason to discuss in the next chapter measures to preempt the return of such evitable populist neo-illiberalism in the future.

Before arguing for historical evitability, I must clarify its meaning, the distinction between historical evitability and inevitability. I propose that the question of historical inevitability turns on the sensitivity of historical events to their initial conditions. History is inevitable when it is insensitive to initial conditions; even if the initial conditions were different, within a wide range of variations, the historically significant result would have remained sufficiently similar to be considered inevitable. History is evitable when it is sensitive to initial conditions. If the initial conditions were a little different, the historically significant event or something similar to it would not have occurred. There are two types of historical inevitability as insensitivity to initial conditions, *historical linearity* and *over-determination* (Ben-Menahem 1997; Tucker 2004, 220–239; Inkpen and Turner 2012; Sterelny 2016). Let me explain.

Historical linearity means simply that large effects have large causes and large causes have large effects. Linear historical processes are inevitable because their effects are not sensitive to small variations in their large causes. For example, once the Soviet Union and the United States joined the Second World War on the side of the British Empire (large causes), the Axis powers could not have won the war (large effects) because of the overwhelming military balance of power aligned against them. Even if many small things were different, if the allies made more or fewer military blunders, if Hitler ordered the attack on the Soviet Union, Operation Barbarossa, to start earlier or postponed it again, the Axis powers would have still lost the war in any such scenario. Some historical failures of social engineering resulted from misunderstanding of how large and linear some processes were, and insensitive to interventions. For example, the attempts to turn Poland into a socialist and atheistic nation, Iraq into a liberal democracy, and Russia into a society governed by the rule of law were doomed to failure because of the linearity of these political aspects of the local cultures.

Another type of historical inevitability results from the *overdetermination* of effects by multiple cause. Each overdetermining cause may be small, but none is necessary. For example, once Caesar entered the forum on the Ides of March, given the number of assassins, his assassination was overdetermined. Even if some of the assassins had second thoughts and others missed him, there were enough assassins determined to kill him. The Industrial Revolution was inevitable in this sense because many innovators and entrepreneurs were working on similar projects. States make mistakes when they do not realize how overdetermined some processes are, and try to change them by minor interventions. For example, many though not all assassinations fail to achieve their political goals because different leaders pursue the same types of policies with similar efficiency under the same constraints, so killing one or more does not change the results of the process. The movie *Munich* makes this point vividly by showing how a series of assassinations brings about only more assassination without any tangible political or strategic change. Assassinating Hitler or Stalin, however, would have changed history non-linearly by saving the lives of millions.

Historical processes that were not linear and/ or overdetermined were evitable. The most non-linear systems are chaotic. Processes that would have turned out entirely differently had things been slightly, even imperceptibly, different, like the proverbial "butterfly effect" when the flapping of butterfly wings in Brazil causes a tornado in Texas, are chaotic, like the weather system. Had history been chaotic, it would have been entirely incomprehensible and unpredictable. A squatter in the Amazon would have burnt a shrub and consequently socialists would have won the elections in Texas, declared independence, and flew to the moon to start a Buddhist commune. History, however, obviously had non-linear junctures: "for want of a nail, the kingdom fell," when small causes had huge effects; for example, when individual decisions affected societies and states, but were not overdetermined. The widely accepted historical counterfactual "No Hitler, no Holocaust' conveys the idea that Hitler's personal obsession with Jews had non-linear effects that were not overdetermined. While many Nazi leaders were complicit in the Holocaust, no other Nazi leader would have likely ordered it. To take a similar example, Colonel Heinz Brandt probably pushed a suitcase under a table on April 20, 1944 and consequently preempted the early end of the Second World War. He did not know that the suitcase contained a bomb that would have killed Hitler and unleashed a military coup d'état that would have probably been successful in ending the Second World War earlier.

Since dictatorships invest much power and authority in a supreme leader, that leader's tiny personal peculiarities can shape history more than the decisions of democratic leaders who must take into consideration voters, lobbyists, special interests, the law, liberal institutions, and so on. The institutions of liberal democracy were designed to reduce the contingencies that follow the investing of inordinate power in one or few leaders. By attempting to deconstruct institutional checks and balances, neo-illiberal democracy makes political history more contingent but also more evitable.

A Contemporary Case for Economic Inevitability

Before arguing for the historical evitability of contemporary neo-illiberal democracy, I want to formulate the strongest case I can for the opposite position, for economically determined, historically inevitable neo-illiberal democracy as a result of the 2008 Great Recession. It would run something like this: As Karl Marx foresaw, capitalism is a wonderful force for innovation, economic growth, and globalization of prosperity through competition and trade. Since the end of the Cold War, the global economy underwent what Richard Baldwin (2016) called *the great convergence* and consequently experienced the greatest reduction in poverty in world history. The gap between the *global* rich and poor has contracted to levels not seen since the eighteenth century, when greater global equality resulted from universal poverty. The cause of greater equality today is the ascent of the global poor to the global middle classes.

While the global economy has grown at a rapid pace as a result of globalization, advanced industrial economies have grown at a slower average pace since about 1970. Though *global* equality increased, equality *within* states, including most advanced industrial economies has decreased. The combination of lower growth and greater inequality created stagnation in the incomes of the middle classes of rich countries while generating rapid growth of the global middle classes, especially in East and South

Asia. Global capitalism is wonderful. But, it has a near fatal and inevitable flaw. It is given to unpredictable and inevitable periodic financial crises and recessions. When capital managers make different mistakes at different times, markets compensate and remain at an overall equilibrium. But, when, *inevitably* sooner or later, they all over-extend credit in more or less the same way at more or less the same time, the global economy keels over. Technocratic and political elites cannot prevent misallocations of credit or effectively reverse them, once it becomes apparent that they happened. Consequently, ordinary people, especially the lower middle classes, who lose most economically and socially from the recession *inevitably* lose trust in democratic elites and liberal technocratic experts. To make things worse, elites react to severe economic downturns with *elite populism*, constructing social floors to keep their families from falling down the social and economic staircase. Looked at from the other side, from the social and economic ground floor, the upper floors look much like ceilings. Whichever way one looks at it, social mobility is blocked. When the economic pie shrinks or stagnates, a larger slice for one must mean a smaller slice for others. In a less than zero-sum game, upward mobility for some necessitates downward mobility for others. Elites then "rig" the rules of the socio-economic game, as Donald Trump on the right and Robert Reich on the left agreed.

When economic stagnation or recession persist, the elite encloses itself in its protected social penthouse. It disables the social elevators, jams the lifts, and barricades the stairs. This short-term elite populism *inevitably* generates popular populism from groups who are pushed downward or whose mobility is blocked. The "revolt of the masses" undermines the foundation of the social structure through populist political extremes. The lower middle classes attempt to imitate the elites by building their own floors to keep themselves from falling even deeper. They push downward those even weaker and more unfortunate than the falling middle classes, especially ethnic groups from different parts of the world who tend on the whole to prefer spicy foods, perhaps because they originate from warmer climates. Alternatively, historically, some of those on the bottom of society, impoverished farmers and unemployed workers, align with the armed intelligentsia on the left to push upwards and sideways to bring the whole social edifice down in a revolution. The working class in advanced industrial economies has been decimated by the expansion of the middle class, services industry, and by automation and outsourcing of manufacturing to countries with lower costs of labor. What is left then is too small and demoralized to embark on a revolution or class struggle. Populist neo-illiberal democracy is the manifestation of the *inevitable* revolt of the lower middle classes.

Prolonged recessions undermine existential, personal, professional, and vocational security and identity. Recessions tend, then, to awaken from their evolutionary slumber parts of the psyche that were useful when our evolutionary ancestors lived in small tribes and became subjected to extreme natural selection, as evolutionary psychologists and anthropologists of the school of René Girard argued at some length. Xenophobia and scapegoating are in this respect like sea sickness. Natural selection did not favor humans, who could withstand long sea voyages, or long-term unemployment, or threats to social status. Some people misinterpret the effects of rough seas or bumps on the road on their inner ears as "being poisoned." The atavistic mechanism then is to vomit. This mechanism was very useful for protecting bodies in the context of eating things that could be poisonous. But, vomiting in cars today is not terribly helpful as a solution to a non-existing problem.

Likewise, when some people sense economic insecurity, they respond by reenacting involuntarily yet inevitably ancient behavioral patterns that must have been conducive to survival hundreds of thousands of years ago, but make little sense in the modern world. They look for a small tribe for protection and reconstruct it as nation, ethnic group, or race. "For most of history, survival was insecure ... cultures tend[ed] to emphasize strong in-group solidarity, conformity to group norms, rejection of outsiders, and obedience to strong leaders. Under extreme scarcity, xenophobia is realistic;... survival becomes a zero sum struggle. Under perceptions of threat, people tend to close ranks behind a strong leader, forming a united front against outsiders – a strategy that can be called the authoritarian reflex" (Norris and Inglehart 2019). Norris and Inglehart's regression analysis connected "survivalist" values that express a sense of existential threat, following the recession to older age cohorts, who tended to vote for neo-illiberals. The younger the cohorts, the more they take survival for granted and are consequently tolerant. Periodic economic recessions push all age cohorts in an authoritarian illiberal direction, but to different degrees. The scapegoating mechanism is a nearly universal human response to collective stresses such as war, hunger, disease, and economic recessions. This mechanism can be found practically in all cultures, as the school of Girard explored at some length.

When people misinterpret their situation as being under existential threat – and obviously it does not take much for many people to construct reality in such terms – people look for a tribe for protection, scapegoats to blame for their troubles, and other tribes to attack, both to ensure group solidarity and increase their share of the food, by excluding weaker members of the in-group and stealing from members of the outgroup. The economically distressed mind reconstructs an ancient drama populated by ghosts of the evolutionary past, projected onto a modern screen. The rest, accusing the victims, as if they poison wells, or spy for the enemy, or destroy the crops, or take away jobs, or are sexual predators and criminals, are rationalizations, justifications for inflicting harm on the weak and defenseless. When the tribe is in danger, chances of survival increase when it is led by a chieftain who lacks empathy and loves risk, and so can sacrifice the few for the survival of the many. Psychopaths are naturally gifted for fulfilling such a role. The result is catastrophic. In the modern globally interlinked world, instead of encouraging and facilitating trade and migration to stimulate the global economy and generate growth and efficiencies that can shorten and moderate the severity of recessions and then boost growth, instinctively people limit them to rely on their own flints and scrapers and conquer the neighboring waterhole.

Once these passionate archaic demons awake and escape their ancient mental genie bottles, *inevitably*, it is impossible to confine them again. Interest, let alone reason, cannot control passions, even when the economy that triggered the atavistic passions is well on its way to recovery and there is less reason for economic anxiety, especially in welfare states. This turns a bad economic situation into a social and political catastrophe. A vicious cycle of economic decline, breakdown of trade and mobility, economic and political hostilities, possesses the body politic, spreads, and infects the whole world. This atavistic mechanism is so contagious because once one group treats others as existential threats, the others start behaving in the same way, and soon enough, for no natural or economic reason, humanity returns to the primordial scene of evolutionary battle for survival, where the psychopaths survive and compassion or morality are deadly vices. This contagion is *inevitable* because nobody has voluntary control over the misinterpretation of modern reality in Stone Age terms.

Historically, such downward economic and political spirals ended in wars. Wars open meritocratic channels for upward mobility; being well connected helps soldiers to "have good wars," survive wars, but not win them. Some members of the old elites die fighting. Others lose their property. A decimated elite can finally absorb social mobility. Wars make space for brave soldiers in the upper echelons. After the war, economic reconstruction creates growth and prosperity. Eventually even the ancient demons tire and go back inside their mental genie bottles to slumber. People feel secure again and even feel comfortable liberalizing trade and migration. A virtuous cycle of increasing prosperity and social and economic openness and progress, democracy and liberalism, comes to dominate. Until the next *inevitably* unexpected financial crisis and recession – and so on and on. Arguably the world economy is now in the fourth or fifth iteration of such a cycle since the French Revolution, itself a reaction to an economic cycle. Karl Marx's mistake then was to impose an eschatological-messianic Judeo-Christian linear progressive narrative on cyclical, economically determined, history. There is no historical equivalent of nirvana. There is no escape from the historical cycle of destruction and rebirth. The Communist or managerial faith in central planning was an illusion that only made things worse because it consistently misallocated capital and blocked innovation, thus generating sustained decline or, at best, low growth, and consequently an even stronger version of the tribal atavistic reaction to perceptions of insecurity, as Stalin demonstrated in force, and the fate of Communist former Yugoslavia should remind sceptics. Communism did not eliminate nationalism as Marx had expected. On the contrary, it strengthened it. The ethnic nation-states in East Europe were constructed by Communists after the Second World War through massive expulsions of populations on the basis of their nationality. The multi-national Communist states, Czechoslovakia, the Soviet Union, and Yugoslavia split according to their nationalities in the immediate aftermath of Communism, at immense humanitarian and economic costs in Yugoslavia.

This inevitable cyclical *ideal eternal history* is independent of human volition. Nobody wills it, yet no one can stop or control it once the passions are triggered. Economically active agents bring it about, whether they like it or not. During recessions, individual members of the elite feel compelled to concentrate wealth and power and use it to block upper mobility. This results in self-destruction. Since behind the thin veneer of civilization people are irrational over-grown simians, when subjected to economic pressure they bypass their rationality, such as it is, and react as though they were under selective evolutionary pressure and turn tribal, xenophobic, authoritarian, and, given the context of the modern industrial global economy, even more self-destructive. Reasoning with people in this state is futile. They are too consumed by passions, fear, and hate to recognize their own self-interest. De Maistre gets his last laugh at the ideals of the Enlightenment; modern democracy commenced with Robespierre and now concludes with Trump, in a *reductio ad absurdum* of democracy as Runciman (2018) put it. History repeats itself first as a tragedy, then as a farce, and finally as a reality show, or a theater of the absurd.

This time, however, the cycle may end differently because, as Runciman (2018) argued, serious wars with many casualties that open channels for mobility and promote egalitarianism and social unity have gone the way of the steam engine and the typewriter. They are off the current political menu and stay off, because of the potential total destruction that modern military technology may unleash. Norris and Inglehart (2019) argued that the most indicative demographic property of neo-illiberals is their advanced age. Old people do not often engage in violence rather than send young men to fight, and do not form militias. The demographic structure of contemporary advanced industrial societies, where there are historically fewer young men as a percentage of the population discourages violence. Young men in economic trouble today rely on their parents more than on peers; it is not common for children to form militias with their parents, though some indeed join fringe right-wing groups, especially in Europe. Small, technology-intensive wars may be possible or even likely, but they do not unify nations, or open channels for mass social mobility, or promote democratic reforms. Instead, they divide nations further against themselves and feed mutual distrust because only a minority participates in modern wars, while the majority pays for them. Holmes (2018) suggested that voters who became populists lost their leverage over their elites when conscription and the Cold War ended. Elites ceased caring for the loyalty of the lower classes. Plausible as this argument may sound, it is certainly not universal, since democracies that maintained conscription were not spared the class cleavage and the consequent rise of populism. To take opposite examples, the Israeli Likud-led government adopted many of the populist themes that dominate East-Central European politics, attacks on the judiciary, scorn for educated cosmopolitan elites, and disrespect for the rights of the Arab minorities and African immigrants, albeit without gerrymandering. In Switzerland, a country with conscription but no enemies, the populist Swiss People's Party is the largest party, with 30 percent of the votes.

What happened?

The above ideal eternal history contains plausible elements. But, as an argument for the historical inevitability of neo-illiberal democracy, it is flawed. History is not ideal but concrete. An obvious exception to the above idealized history is the Indian voters for the neo-illiberal BJP. Their demographics are similar to those of voters for liberal parties in developed countries. They tend to be socially mobile middle and upper-economic classes and established immobile-by-definition members of upper castes, more urban, better educated and, according to some analysis, younger. While these voters acknowledged their mobility and better economic conditions, they also felt that their employment opportunities had deteriorated before 2014. The populist frustration of the Indian middle classes may not result from their actual mobility, but in relation to their expectations and aspirations (Sridharan 2017). They may have felt that a corrupt political elite associated with the Congress Party has been taxing them to pay for a patronage system and subsidies for the poor and ethnic minorities. Other specifically Indian factors may well be at play.

However, to understand why neo-illiberal democracy happened, we need to do first what historians do, ask why a concrete event happened. The causes that answer the "why question" depend on how the question is framed, as well as on the evidence.

There is an old joke about a centenarian couple who announce that they have decided to divorce. People ask why? The couple reply that they were waiting for their grandchildren to die. The answer frames the question as "why did you decide to divorce *now* when you are a hundred years old, rather than when you were younger?" The answer explains what changed recently, the grandchildren died, so nobody close would be hurt from the split. Most historiographic causal explanations frame the question they answer as a comparison between two situations: one brought about the interesting effects, and the other did not. They ask what distinguished the one from the other. The comparison can be between two succeeding states as in the joke about the centenarians. But it can also be simultaneous: for example, it may be possible to ask the centenarian couple why they decided to divorce, whereas the couple in the next apartment in the retirement home did not. The couple can explain that the other couple is 101 years old, so they are too old. Another comparison can be between what could have been changed, was humanly manipulable, and what was not. For example, if we ask for a causal explanation of a forest fire, we would mention a discarded match but not the presence of oxygen in the air and trees in the forest. Nobody can do anything about oxygen in the air and trees in the forest, but the person who discarded a lit match carelessly could have easily preempted the fire (Tucker 2004, 185–207).

The question about neo-illiberal democracy that I think is most on people's mind is Hillary Clinton's: "*What happened?*": A question that expresses surprise that can be reframed as "Why did this happen suddenly *now*?" What changed *in the second decade of the twenty-first century* after seventy years of liberal democratic consensus and hegemony in Western Europe and North America? Few seem to ask: Why not Canada? At least few outside of Canada.

It is quite obvious and not very controversial or original that a major part of "what happened" is the global Great Recession of 2007–2009 and the anemic recovery in North America and Europe. The Great Recession did not have immediate political effects. Nor did it affect all countries and all sectors in each country equally. Many different local factors intervened to affect the results. The political effects of the recession worked their way through different channels that generated a time lapse with intermediary variables connecting the economic recession with its political effects. Uncoincidentally, the same held for the previous global economic recessions and its political effects. The Nazis gained power four years after the onset of the Great Depression.

The factors that mediated between the recession and illiberalism were not simple forms of economic misery. As Stockemer et al. (2018) and Norris and Inglehart (2019) showed, there is only a weak correlation between illiberal populist voting patterns and workers with low incomes, blue-collar manufacturing workers, and voters with concerns about inequality. The illiberal power base is never among those who suffer most economically. The poorest of the poor have a strong interest in supporting and expanding the welfare state, not in dismantling its liberal institutions, and they do not always participate in political processes. In the United States and other diverse states the poorest tend to be members of minorities (African-American, Roma-Gypsy in Hungary, Arabs in Israel). Minorities have an interest in opposing illiberal democrats who govern for the majority against the minority and do not respect their rights. When they vote, they tend not to vote for illiberals.

The one definite contribution that this populist neo-illiberal decade has already made to political science is its direct refutation of modernization theory, the causal association of the probability that democracies survive with high average gross national product (Przeworski et al. 2000). *All* the countries where neo-illiberals won democratic elections, participated in governing coalitions, or at least gained a significant share of the vote, with the exception of India, were theoretically too rich to have had such challenges to democracy. Prosperous welfare states, where the state cares for its citizens from cradle to grave and where it is almost impossible to fall through the social safety networks, such as in Scandinavia, have some of the most virulent and powerful populist illiberal parties in Europe. Obviously, there is no rational economic reason for Norwegian or Danish populist neo-illiberalism. Some suggest welfare anxiety, fear of competition over welfare transfers with poor immigrants. This explanation must assume that the immigrants are more unemployed and welfare dependent than natives. But immigrant welfare dependence is constructed when welfare states prohibit them from working and paying taxes. Welfare dependence is an effect of xenophobia at least as much as it is a cause.

Since there is no simple linear correlation between populism or neo-illiberalism and poverty, Mounk suggested that the intermediate variable is economic *anxiety* rather than actual *distress*. Founded or unfounded *fears* for the future rather than *actual misery*, unemployment, loss of home, or poverty, caused neo-illiberalism. Affluence without growth dampens expectations for the future and leads to anxiety. Workers with below average education and residents of rural areas who possess weak economic bargaining positions with employers and economic prospects sense this angst particularly acutely (Mounk 2018, 134–160). Holmes (2018) agreed that the economic explanation for the decline in democracy is insecurity, fear of downward mobility, and blocked mobility, not egalitarian resentment of inequality. The rise of populist illiberalism globally correlates strongly with blocked mobility. The factor that seems to correlate more significantly than economic variables with populism is absence of mobility.

Accordingly, I argue that two types of processes followed the Great Recession in all the countries that developed neo-illiberalism. These processes generated, after a time lapse, populist neo-illiberalism to different degrees and in different varieties because of myriad local factors:

1 The mental misconstruction of the prolonged economic recession in modern economies as an evolutionary extinction event that triggered archaic passions that led to authoritarianism, xenophobia, and scapegoating. This factor does not lead necessarily or inevitably to neo-illiberalism.
2 The elites reacted passionately to negative or low economic growth, by solidifying a rigid class structure, protected by extreme constraints on social mobility. This short-term self-destructive elite populism generated an equally populist backlash-illiberal populism.

These two processes reinforced each other. The elite's "hoarding of opportunities," caused those below them in the social hierarchy to feel socially and economically trapped, thus contributing further to the misinterpretation of their situation as an evolutionary extinction event. Elite and popular populism fed on each other in vicious circles.

Since I have already elaborated on the first process, I examine here the second. Americans have always been more tolerant of inequality than many Europeans, since they had faith in equality of opportunity (Reves 2017, 58). This faith has always been a bit exaggerated. The aftermath of the recession turned the faithful into sceptics, and the sceptics into heretics who believe the social "game" is rigged. Populism expresses *class resentment* (when we understand class loosely as rigidly strong correlations between wealth, social status, health, domicile, education, occupation, and those of one's children and parents) against the upper middle class but not against wealth and inequality (cf. Reeves 2017, 18–19). The class divisions between the upper middle classes and other classes have been growing since before the recession (Murray 2012; Fishkin 2014; Reeves 2017). However, the recession contributed decisively to the reinforcement and sealing of the class glass and concrete ceilings and floors.

Social scientists distinguish *absolute mobility* from *relative mobility*. "Absolute mobility is a measure of whether you are economically better off than your parents were at the same age ... Relative mobility is a measure of which rung of the ladder you stand on in your generation, compared to the rung your parents stood on in their own generation" (Reeves 2017, 59). Historically, there have been high levels of absolute mobility in advanced industrial countries. So much so, that those whose relative mobility was slow agreed to tolerate it for the greater good of absolute mobility. The comparison with socialist economies in Communist countries, where there were initially high levels of relative mobility, was instructive because even those who survived the terror and purges that generated the high relative mobility enjoyed only slow absolute mobility. Many people in Communist countries concluded that they preferred Western absolute mobility to Eastern relative mobility. The American and West European lower middle classes clearly lived better than the upper classes of socialist bureaucracies. They not only had higher purchasing powers, but also had better health, greater longevity, higher education, better lifestyle, more leisure, and so on.

Recession means economic contraction – there are fewer economic goods to distribute. Fewer economic agents, workers, managers, entrepreneurs, and so on are required to produce them. Under such conditions, absolute mobility, which is usually a more than zero sum game from which all can benefit, is possible only when one's parents are really poor. Downward absolute mobility becomes a real possibility even in advanced industrial economies. When the economy does not grow, absolute mobility for some must come at the expense of downward mobility for others. The gap between absolute and relative mobility disappears. Suddenly, absolute mobility requires also relative mobility, and relative mobility becomes scarce because of the resistance of elites to their own downward mobility, necessary for the upward mobility of others. The disappearance of the gap between absolute and relative mobility takes time to be apparent and tangible, and some of its victims may wait patiently for economic growth to resume and, with it, absolute mobility. When they lose patience and faith in future absolute mobility, the populist hour arrives.

Prior to the recession, for sixty years of economic growth with few interruptions, the elites had larger slices of the economic pie, while still leaving enough for others to nibble on, and not just crumbs. When the pie contracted, merely keeping the size of the slice constant necessitates taking pie from the mouths of others and limiting their access to the pie pan. This is what I referred to earlier as *elite populism*. To protect their passions for a sense of entitlement, vanity, social status, and power, and satisfy greed, upper-middle-class elites blocked mobility and consequently endangered the free market liberal democratic order that allowed them to obtain and sustain their considerable advantages and privileges. In previous reiterations of this kind of elite populism the result was the destruction of the elite in war, revolution, or civil strife.

The elite's populist passion for maintaining their economic and social status at the expense of the mobility of those lower down the slippery social pole, contributed to the generation of the political mass populism of the lower-middle and middle-middle classes. The elites do not block the mobility of the lower classes because the middle classes separate them. Conversely, the poor do not resent the upper middle classes because they do not block them and pay for transfer payments to them. The middle and especially the lower middle classes resent transfer payments to those less fortunate than themselves because they feel like their upper-middle-class enemies, who do not mind paying for welfare, force them to pay for people who are not considerably worse off than themselves, but with whom they do not identify or empathize. Obviously, the Affordable Care Act (Obamacare) was interpreted in such terms by lower-middle-class Americans who had not had health insurance and were forced to subsidize poor Americans. This led to the emergence of the populist "Tea Party" and the Democratic Party defeat in the 2010 mid-term elections.

This revolt of the middle classes against distribution seems to be universally true of all the neo-illiberal parties and movements. For example, even in India, the 2014 vote for the neo-illiberal BJP was fueled partly by middle-class resentment against affirmative action policies for lower castes and assistance to the rural poor (Chatterji et al. 2019, 8–9).

The distinctive feature of current populism is that the popular neo-illiberal populists do not hate or express *anger* against the elites, as much as *resentment*. Hate is directed at a class of people for what they are, not for what they did, and seeks their elimination, erasure, obliteration. Hate is reserved now for those weaker and lower on the social hierarchy, immigrants, and ethnic minorities, who are too weak to retaliate. Anger, by contrast, is for particular slights and can be directed only at somebody comparable to oneself with whom getting even is imaginable. *The populist masses hate the foreigners because they cannot imagine being angry at their elites.* The elites are too socially remote for imagining retaliation against them. The populist masses admire the populist leaders who hail from the elite because they can express anger and derision at members of the elites – their peers, which they themselves could not dare nor imagine expressing.

Elster (1999) investigated the transmutations of emotions, how socially unacceptable passions are transmuted into other less unacceptable passions or are rationalized as interests. Hate is a socially unacceptable passion. Popular populists and their demagogues transmuted it into a more acceptable passion for "revenge" against the socially weak for fictional slights. They construct foreigners as criminals, rapists, and so on, despite the overwhelming evidence that immigrants are considerably less prone to crime than natives. *Frustrations and fears from blocked social mobility are transmuted into hate, and hate is transmuted into passion for revenge that generates narratives of victimization that justify inflicting suffering and attempting to eliminate strangers who hurt no one.* Welcome to the human race!

Hate may also transmute into rationalized economic interest, alleged competition over jobs. Overwhelming economic evidence, and the very success of countries founded on mass migrations, proves that economic competition with immigrants, if at all, appears temporarily in specific industries and then disappears quickly as the immigrants consume what they earn, and generate demand for labor, while offering themselves as labor supply. As workers gravitate toward the niches that offer them the highest compensations, immigrants too move on from the worst-paid jobs, in which under current conditions, the populist masses are hardly interested. The populist lower middle classes do not rush to pick strawberries in California, tomatoes in Southern Italy, and white asparagus in Germany. Nor are they excited by the prospects of washing incontinent elderly patients who suffer from dementia. Entrepreneurial immigrants like Carnegie and Tesla, Sergey Brin of Google, and Elon Musk, created whole industries and millions of jobs, absolute and relative mobility for the masses. Immigration restrictions will not loosen the blocks on social mobility, but block opportunities for mobility that immigrants may open (cf. Guest 2011).

Rigid class structure with a self-serving elite explains political passivity and indifference, and consequent abstention from voting and membership of political parties. If citizens, especially those young and liberal, consider politics to be an insider's competition between elite factions that share indifference to the interests and concerns of ordinary people like themselves, they have no interest in participating in a game in which they have no stake and from which they have nothing to gain. The end of social mobility also explains the resentment of voters against politicians whom they perceive as having reached their positions through membership of the elite, rather than merit. The establishment candidates in the US 2016 presidential elections were the wife, and the son and brother, of former presidents. The winning populist formula is for a leader to be a turncoat member of the elite, who can turn against his peers to expresses hate and anger, without transgressing accepted social barriers. The populist leader becomes, then, a "tribune of the plebs," somebody who voices the passions the plebs cannot express because of social inequalities. Insults against fellow members of the elite go down well with the populist base. Scapegoating hateful weak minorities is even better in demonstrating that the populist leader, though a member of the elite, is still one of the mob. Societies that are riven by class or caste can then unite against helplessly weak minorities (Chatterji et al. 2019, 9).

Different populisms resent different elites that use different methods to block social mobility. Fishkin (2014) noted that inequality in the nineteenth century resulted from unequal access to capital. It was true again after the end of Communism in East Europe when the old nomen-klatura still controlled the banks in societies where private accumulation of capital had been close to impossible for decades. Inequality in the United States today, explained Fishkin, results from unequal access to education. Class resentment is directed, then, against what Fishkin (2014) called class "bottlenecks," most notably against the formally educated, and education in general.

The global popularity and political significance of *The Apprentice* as a launching platform for political careers demonstrate that for many people working for a tough but fair boss who rewards merit and hard work with mobility has become a fantasy. Trump's case is obvious, but other similar participants in this and similar reality shows who transmuted their stardom into political careers include the prime minister of Georgia Lado Gurgenidze, the Mayor of Brazil's largest city São Paulo, João Doria, Finnish parliament member Harry Harkimo, Danish EU MP Klaus Riskær Pedersen, Slovak politician Nora Mojsejová, politically influential Lord Alan Sugar in the UK, and Bram Moszkowicz in the Netherlands. *Dragons' Den, a* similar reality show, where entrepreneurs rather than employees compete, led similarly to political careers for some of its judges, such as the Czech populist illiberal xenophobic politician Tomio Okamura. In the early-modern period there was a literary genre that came to be known as "food pornography," texts about elaborate feasts that reflect a society with literate hungry people. *The Apprentice* and similar reality television shows can similarly be called "mobility pornography." The viewers of *The Apprentice* fantasize about *joining* rather than *hanging* the international capitalists. They respect and accept the legitimacy of plutocrats, entrepreneurs, and managers because they believe they climbed to the top fairly without blocking the mobility of others. They reject the legitimacy of the upper middle classes, experts, professionals, academics, and intellectuals.

Populists naturally resent the codes of upper-middle-class educated politeness that are used to exclude them. In the nineteenth century, upper classes distinguished themselves by knowing how to dress, how to address social superiors and inferiors, avoid cursing in public, keep personal hygiene, blow their noses and wipe their mouths in handkerchiefs and napkins rather than use their sleeves, and use cutlery properly, distinguish fish from meat knives and so on. By now, these norms have been equalized. Almost no adult still uses their sleeves to clean but alas few still use fish knives. Instead, the upper middle classes have invented speech codes to distinguish the educated upper classes from their uncouth moral inferiors.

The norms of verbal politeness associated with "political correctness" are parts of upper-middle-class socialization. Maybe the upper middle classes are less racist and sexist than other classes, or maybe they know better than to talk about it. But speech codes can flush out the lower-middle-class boy who repeats something he heard at home perhaps without quite understanding what it means or reflecting on it. Hatred of the lower classes can transmute then into passion for revenge that justified social exclusion. Then, when a populist politician deliberately and nonchalantly breaks all the codes of upper-middle-class politeness, he demonstrates to the excluded lower classes that he is on their side, while burning bridges to the elite by performing speech acts that would forever exclude the populist from polite society, like telling an authority figure in public to go and fuck themselves (to borrow Woody Allen's line from the 1976 movie *The Front*). Of course, political correctness speech codes are not used exclusively for excluding people who were not brought up by upper-middle-class parents or educational institutions: they are also used as regulatory weapons in power struggles *within* the upper middle classes when some faction accuses the other of being incorrect, and the other faction returns the compliment. Some people may genuinely believe that political correctness is an aspect of social justice, as fish knives really are better for dealing with fish bones. But within the populist political discourse it is perceived as a class shibboleth and then manipulated by upper-class demagogues to display their credentials.

Class divisions in post-Communist countries have different origins and different characteristics, but have become rigid, following the 2008 recession. The 1989 political revolutions did not develop into social revolutions. The late Communist elite traded its political power for economic power and then used it to affect politics by incorporating new political elites. The Hungarian and Polish populists were credible anti-elitists because they were staunchly anti-Communist in societies with strong correlations between class and membership in the late-Communist nomenklatura. The neo-illiberal populists appeared immune to incorporation by the late Communist elite through corruption, like other politicians, either because they appeared fanatically anti-Communist, or because they appeared too rich to be corruptible. As established politicians, they were also members of the elite, and so were credible tribunes of the plebs.

The two intermediary effects of the recession, misinterpretation of the economic recession as an extinction event and the blocking of social mobility, *favored* populist illiberal democracy almost globally. This accounts for the various manifestations of neo-illiberal populism in countries that otherwise share little. But myriad other local factors participated in preempting or encouraging the electoral successes of neo-illiberal parties, and their abilities to eviscerate and deconstruct liberal institutions. Some small and even random factors affected non-linearly the results, next.

Contingencies

Despite the large linear causes that followed the recession, very small, even minute, differences in initial conditions could have led to entirely different political results. Understanding these historical contingencies is useful, not just for avoiding the conclusion that periodic civilizational breakdown is the inevitable destiny of all free-market liberal democracies, but more importantly for designing institutions to better withstand the kind of self-destructive pressures that economic recessions generate and will continue to generate, as shown in the next chapter.

The short history of recent populist neo-illiberal democracy had at least three non-linear pivotal turning points that could have easily turned out differently. At each of these junctures, neo-illiberalism could have been preempted: Orbán's dismantling of the liberal institutions of Hungary, the British plebiscite on Brexit, and Trump's presidential victory. These three pivotal events were highly contingent compared, for example, to Putin's restoration of authoritarianism in Russia, which was linear, given his hold over the levers of power and overdetermined in the absence of civic society and liberal institutions in Russia. Each of these three subsequent contingent pivotal junctures exponentially increased the neo-illiberal contagion. Politicians, like other entrepreneurs, imitate successful models, so they spread quickly. For example, once Mussolini developed a successful political model and demonstrated its durability, other politicians rushed to reproduce it by imitation, including all its trappings from the party-state model to military-style uniforms with dark shirts. The model also adapted to local conditions. The same held for Marxist–Leninist regimes during decolonization. The significance of a new political phenomenon is not just in its size and immediate local geopolitical significance, but in becoming a model for imitation, a source of contagion.

Hungary

When Orbán won the Hungarian elections in 2010 for a second non-contiguous term as prime-minster as the head of the 1989 vintage Fidesz party, there was no particular reason for alarm. He had been a prime minister before as a conservative liberal, and the reformed Communist government he and Fidesz replaced was corrupt to the bone, and boasted shamelessly about it. But, when Orbán used Fidesz's parliamentary supermajority to dismantle Hungary's fragile liberal institutions, he met no resistance from outside of Hungary, for example from the European Union and its member states, or from fellow NATO members. Hungary is a small nation of ten million, among the poorest in the European Union, on its Eastern margins, with a non-Indo-European language that few outsiders can comprehend. It is understandable that older and larger traditional liberal democracies were not interested in its system of government. Its main significance for European interests was as a source for cheap skilled labor, especially for German car manufacturing. It was easy to believe that with time and European integration, Hungary would revert to the European mean and rejoin its progressive timeline. But the possibility of contagion, that what started in Budapest would spread to Warsaw and then to London and Washington did not occur to anybody.

Europe could easily have intervened to preempt contagion. It was reasonable to expect that contagion could spread, at least to similar countries that had weak liberal institutions, totalitarian or authoritarian legacies, and resentful, disillusioned, and angry populist electorates. The European Union could have moved decisively to protect the liberal institutions, for example by conditioning subsidies that have been bankrolling Hungary's political patronage regime on adhering to European liberal norms. Since Hungary has no natural resources like Russia or Saudi Arabia, it does not suffer from the political natural resource curse. Instead, it is dependent on subsidies from the European Union and on foreign direct investment, mostly from Germany, and on exports mostly to the EU. European leaders could have leveraged the imbalance of political and economic power to isolate neo-illiberalism once it emerged, preempt its contagion, and put pressure to reverse it, rather than wait and hope. Germany's car manufacturers (which in Germany's corporatist system are close to the government) are responsible for a third of Hungary's exports. They could have threatened to relocate from a legally unsafe illiberal environment to safer countries.

This is particularly frustrating given the effective pressure the European Union exerted later on Greece's left-wing rhetorical populists to preempt "left-wing populist" contagion to Spain and elsewhere. The EU, and especially Germany, adopted a tough negotiation position with Greece and did not give an inch, for fear of left-wing populist contagion. That fear was not of an erosion of liberal democracy but of economic irresponsibility, ballooning government debts, and defaults. A similar political approach may well have preempted the Hungarian contagion. At the same time, American disinterest in the poorer members of the European Union also facilitated the emergence of illiberalism in the old continent. Orbán's illiberalism was protected on the EU level by the ideologically proximate Bavarian Christian Democrats. An American intervention could have overcome the Bavarian objections. But the Obama administration simply did not care enough.

Neo-illiberalism could have been stopped in Hungary, before Poland's PiS party, the Slovaks and the Czechs, and then Austrians and Italian parties witnessed its success and endurance, and ventured to imitate Orbán's policies and the Hungarian model, as indeed the Poles and Austrian populist neo-illiberals admitted publicly. Preempting the Hungarian contagion would have been cheap. But nobody understood what was at stake, and nobody cared.

The American geopolitical retreat from Europe under president Obama, even before Trump's ideological isolationism, allowed the Russians to try to fill in the vacuum and develop and refine their tradecraft of backing radical anti-liberal movements from all the political extremes, irrespective of ideology to magnify internal cleavages within and between European countries, which could lead to breaking down the Western democratic alliances. Orbán's second victory in 2010 and the democratic backslide that followed, Zeman's election as Czech president as populist with Russian backing in 2013, and the financial support of Russia to extremist parties such as the French National Front, took place not just without overt US intervention, but with marked US disinterest in those European countries and in policies that did not have direct economic effect on the United States. As much as the Spanish Civil War was a general rehearsal for the Second World War, the Russian interventions in European politics during Putin's second term as president were general rehearsals for the Russian intervention in the elections in the Western core. The whole adventure must not have cost the Russians more than a few million euros and required the simple insight that to win in majority electoral systems it is not necessary to win a majority if the opposition can be divided, especially by radicalizing politics and pushing it to the extremes. The United States could have afforded to more than match the Russians by supporting opposite political forces, centrist, unifying, and consensus building, and encouraging alliances between centrist forces.

Brexit

Though illiberal governments had assumed power in Hungary and Poland before the Brexit vote in the summer of 2016, Brexit signaled that the populist wave had reached the Western core. The global significance of the plebiscite has far exceeded its domestic political significance within the UK as far as the themes of this book are concerned: The UK was, and will remain, a liberal democracy within or without the European Union. British liberal institutions are probably sufficiently strong and entrenched to check neo-illiberal governments. However, the ultimate populist illiberal democratic tool, the plebiscite, and its populist result demonstrated both that even the oldest liberal democracy is vulnerable to populism and that political changes that had been considered unimaginable have entered the realm of possibility. Brexit encouraged, inspired, and boosted the morale of neo-illiberals everywhere, though Brexit itself is populist but neither illiberal nor liberal.

Brexit did not have to happen; it was neither linearly caused nor overdetermined. The British parliamentary and liberal institutions would have been robust enough to preempt a contingent result like Brexit, had they not been radically undermined from above. The decision to hold a neo-illiberal democratic plebiscite that would bypass the ancient British institutions and norms was prime minister David Cameron's "gambler's ruin"; he believed he had a sure thing, bet the farm on it, and lost everything. Brexit has been entirely contingent on this decision. Another prime minister could have continued to tolerate a Eurosceptic wing of the Conservative Party and the loss of some votes to UKIP that would have harmed the Conservatives but would not have brought UKIP closer to power. The British liberal tradition of government does not include plebiscites, for good reasons. Plebiscites oversimplify complex issues and appeal to the raw passions of voters. The English who voted against the European Union had irreconcilable political agendas and different party affiliations. Some wanted a deregulated Singapore on the Northern Sea if they could only gain export markets; failing to gain free trade agreements, their only plan B would have to be the resurrecting of the British Empire or at least the reconquering of India. Others, wanted Little England without foreigners, Polish plumbers, and food foreigners and more than a few locals would find edible. Still others would have voted in protest for anything that would have upset what they perceive as "the establishment," from abolishing the monarchy to replacing "God save the Queen" as a national anthem with the Sex Pistols' version. Any vote that would not have oversimplified the issues into a "yes" or "no" choice without details would have fragmented the Brexit vote.

Trump

As the election of president Trump with a substantial minority of the votes was very close, many jointly sufficient and individually necessary conditions had to combine to generate the result. Had fewer people believed that Clinton would win without their votes, had the Green Party not run in Pennsylvania, Michigan, and Wisconsin, had Clinton campaigned in the Midwest, had members of the republican leadership come out publicly to call upon republicans not to vote for Trump and either stay at home or vote for a third candidate like the Libertarian Gary Johnson or for Clinton, had Stormy and Donald's other special friends come out before the elections, had the Democrats elected a more electable candidate, had a few young voters bothered to leave home to vote, had the weather been different, and so on ad infinitum and ad nauseam, it could have ended differently.

The contingency of political results on electoral systems is evident in the different outcomes of very similar distributions of neo-illiberal versus liberal votes in different countries. Similar electoral inputs generated very different representative democratic outputs. A substantial minority of votes decided the US presidential election. The populist neo-illiberal Austrian candidate for the presidency lost with an almost identical minority percentage of votes to the one that led Trump to victory. If the United States had an Austrian or French electoral system with two rounds, Trump and Clinton would have faced each other without alternative choices. If only most of the Green voters in Michigan, Wisconsin, and Pennsylvania went in such a second round for what they may have considered the lesser evil, the United States would have had a second President Clinton. Even in Hungary where Fidsz won a 53 percent absolute majority of the votes in 2010, it was transmuted into more than two-thirds majority in the parliament that allowed it to change the constitution and impose neo-illiberalism. In majority systems, a minority party can win elections if its opponents are divided. This leads to a clear strategy for neo-illiberal democrats, who only need to divide their opponents in order to rule. An even smaller minority of votes than Trump's gave absolute parliamentary majority to anti-liberal populists in Poland,

and an even smaller minority of 31 percent gave India's neo-illiberal BJP absolute parliamentary majority in India's first past the post majority electoral system in 2014.

This contingency of results on many non-linear factors demonstrates that neo-illiberalism was not, and is not inevitable, and hence avoidable and pre-emptible, as we discuss next.

5

New Liberalism
without Nostalgia

Economic recessions may not be inevitable. But if they are evitable, political theorists do not possess the special wisdom that would be needed to stop them. For now, we have to assume that economic recessions happen and indeed will continue to happen. Historical experience teaches that once the populist genies are set free, it is quite difficult to confine them again. We can expect a century of Orbán and Trump imitators. The next ones may be just as ruthless, but more intelligent. Still, some populist and neo-illiberal political consequences may be evitable. I argued in the previous chapter for the contingency and evitability of the current crisis of liberal democracy. Accordingly, it is possible to consider reforms that may preempt another self-destructive political reaction when this and the coming economic cycles result in recessions. The reforms that followed the Great Depression and the Second World War preserved and expanded liberal democracy in North America and much of Europe, and moderated the effects of the economic crisis in whose political echoes we live. Lessons from the current crisis could moderate if not preempt the next one.

I have argued that the economic recession triggered populist neo-illiberalism through two mutually reinforcing processes: the constructive misinterpretation of the economic recession as an archaic extinction event; and elite populism that blocks social mobility and thereby generates popular populism. Once they win elections, the ability of populist neo-illiberals to deconstruct the liberal edifice of the state depends on the strengths of the foundations and structures of the liberal institutions, their design, history, and the people who compose them. Accordingly, I propose three groups of preemptive measures: measures designed to prevent the misinterpretations of recessions as evolutionary extinction events; measures designed to facilitate, increase, and promote social mobility even under conditions of economic stagnation or contraction; and measures to strengthen liberal institutions to better withstand and resist illiberal assaults.

To be clear, I do not have policies or activities to offer that may bring contemporary neo-illiberalism to an end, but they may not be necessary. Populism, by its very nature, is self-destructive. Neo-illiberal politicians elected by populists must play a delicate game to survive: They must satisfy the populist passions without self-destructing, for example, with incendiary rhetoric, while not acting on that rhetoric. If they promise to derail international trade and block immigration, they have to maintain trade and some level of immigration to keep the economy from collapsing. They must appear belligerent, while avoiding serious wars. The illiberal populist leader is always in danger of ensnarling himself in his own rhetoric. If they fail, in the aftermath of an economic or military populist debacle, historically, people became more receptive to political innovations.

The opposite scenario is of prudent or lucky neo-illiberals who succeed in avoiding succumbing to the populist passions by outwitting their voters in order to generate increasingly prosperous, urban, and educated populations. Over time, prosperity may create opportunities for liberal restoration. For example, Spain's dictator Franco made some wise decisions – most notably to stay out of the Second World War – and then was lucky because of the Cold War. He opened Spain to global trade and tourism that modernized the country. When he died, Spain smoothly became the liberal democracy it is today. If technocratic illiberalism manages to contain populism, it may not end with a catastrophic bang, but with a whimper of relief, and opportunities for political reform.

Beyond the immediate future, longer and slower trends that some of the authors writing on the current crisis have referred to may open possibilities that seem unlikely in the current political context. For example, for almost two millennia, dominant interpretations of the Judeo-Christian traditions imposed the view that homosexuality was unnatural and immoral. Just a decade or two ago, the mere idea that same-sex marriages would be legally sanctioned, and that an openly gay man married to another man would be a leading candidate for the presidency of the United States, would have seemed outlandish or utopian. The kind of blue-sky political reforms I propose here may seem almost as unrealistic as a gay president with a husband did a decade or two ago.

Finally, since non-linear minute causes participated in bringing about neo-illiberal political outcomes that would have seemed absurd just a decade ago, like the presidency of Donald Trump, other minute non-linear causes that cannot be detected or even imagined today may have similarly surprising results. In countries like the United States, Poland, and Israel, the populist neo-illiberal trend may peak, and may begin to slowly reverse itself. As the President of Israel, Reuven Rivlin put it in his speech at the opening session of Israel's Knesset on October 3, 2019: "The outcomes of the elections constitute a certificate of honor to Israeli society. They are a [football] red card issued by the citizens of Israel to … populism, to a political strategy that nourished itself from rummaging in social fissures. It considers our collective fears a resource it may manipulate to exploit. The election campaign is the most expensive reality show. You should remember that from season to season its rating may plunge, though the results may remain the same."

If and when liberal democrats regain power, they will face the task of instituting preemptive reforms. My recommendations are distinct and perhaps exceptional in being thoroughly *non*-nostalgic. Specifically, I avoid three popular types of nostalgia: Obviously, I have little sympathy for the *mythical* unspecific nostalgia of populist neo-illiberals to some good and great old days. This nostalgia is too vacuous to argue against.

A second type of nostalgia is *social-democratic*, to the golden thirty years that followed the Second World War in Europe. European social democracy then generated robust economic growth, accompanied by social security, and considerably greater social equality and mobility than before the Second World War. Increasing prosperity generated labor shortages that were resolved by mass immigration initiated by governments, which resulted in multi-ethnic and multi-cultural societies. During many of those golden thirty years, Europeans kept benefitting economically from colonialism that also generated social mobility. Those thirty years were not exactly golden for Africa or Asia. In the United States, Southern racism disenfranchised and oppressed many of its citizens. Everywhere, including in Europe, rights of women and some minorities were not as respected as they are today. The good old days are remembered as such, especially against the background of some of the worst horrors in human history that immediately preceded them. The Second World War left Europe more equal because of the destruction of wealth. The baseline of 1945, the year zero, generated high growth because it was so low. These factors cannot and indeed should not be replicated. European Social Democracy faltered because it could not keep delivering rapid economic growth without compromising on the quality of social services. There are many possible reasons for this crisis, from the energy crisis, to decolonization, to new technologies, to the very unprecedented prosperity that made it difficult for the economies to sustain their previous rates of growth. Whatever these causes were, clearly the world has not and cannot, and perhaps should not, revert to its pre-1973 state. If a return to 1970 were feasible, some nostalgic country would have achieved it by now.

The crises of social democracy in the 1970s led to the democratic elections of parties that advocated the sacrifice of equality for the restoration of economic growth. Though the transition was painful for some, the booming second half of the 1980s and 1990s, with the political certainties that accompanied the fall of the Berlin Wall and "the end of history" have generated another political nostalgia. Though the new wealth was not distributed equally, by the late 1990s, the high point of success of these liberalizing policies, it seemed like all the social boats rose in the economic tide, though not to the same height. The liberalizing economic model was particularly successful globally, where it not only raised global rates of growth, but also increased global equality, since much of the growth took place in the poorer developing world. Global growth benefitted advanced industrial countries, too, by increasing their purchasing power of imports.

The apparent success of this model had some external causes; most notably, the peace dividend from the end of the Cold War would have benefitted the Northern hemisphere, irrespective of economic policies, though Russia has benefitted from this dividend just as much as NATO countries, with somewhat less impressive results. But then came the Great Recession that resulted in negative and then slow growth that caused temporarily a decrease in inequality in advanced industrial countries, as the values of the assets of the rich depreciated. As global growth resumed, advanced industrial economies experienced growing inequality combined with economic stagnation; this violated the bargain of the 1980s, higher growth and mobility at the expense of equality. The failures of the twenty-first century were not entirely the results of economic liberalism: Terrorism and the costly military overreaction to it had nothing to do with economic liberalization. But the Great Recession and the failure of elites not only to preempt it, but to end it quickly and restart rapid growth with or without equality generated nostalgia for the days when the model worked so well that it had the soft power to destabilize and topple competing types of regimes.

Irving Kristol founded neo-conservatism by describing it as "conservatism without nostalgia." At that time conservatives had more reasons to be nostalgic than liberals. Now, liberals should learn that lesson, and become new-liberals, without nostalgia. The real and imaginary pasts of nostalgia are neither possible nor desirable. Since many popular policy alternatives or solutions to neo-illiberal democracy are nostalgic, the following ideas are on the innovative cutting edge. My recommendations are based on the previous analysis and are not local or state-specific but general and theoretical. Some of the ideas may be balloons that explode upon hitting the political stratosphere, while others will prove to be politically heavier than air and remain on the ground. I hope some ideas, however, will lead to intercontinental flights of reason. Finally, I present some ideas about the meaning of new-liberalism without nostalgia. To be clear, I am not offering here a theory of liberal justice or a vision of liberal utopia. Rather, I propose how to preempt neo-illiberal democracy and what kind of new liberalism may be most effective, nothing more. There is voluminous literature on liberalism and justice and I have nothing to add to it.

Preempting Populism

Populism is a political reflection of existential fear. This fear drives all the rest, the hate, scapegoating, and illiberalism. It is possible that the fear could be preempted or stopped by assuring personal security.

Social security and the welfare state were designed in reaction to the Great Depression, to prevent the adverse effects of extreme poverty and as a Keynesian mean to create a floor for aggregate demand that should limit the bottom side of any recession. These measures passed the test of "our" Great Recession of 2008–2009. Indeed, this time there was no hunger, or *increased* homelessness (though some people lost their homes) or families in rags begging for food in the streets, no *new* soup kitchens and no shanty towns. However, social security and welfare failed to do what they were not designed to do: they did not sufficiently reduce existential anxiety and loss of self-esteem and personal identity and dignity. It is necessary, then, to introduce new innovative programs designed to assure more than economic survival and provide more than a safety net.

Universal Basic Income

Guaranteed universal basic income (UBI), unconditional equal transfer payments to all, may be a radical new fear-preempting social program. It would not be cheap, but it may well be cheaper than the costs of populism and neo-illiberalism. Silicon Valley entrepreneurs like UBI plan to facilitate automating disruptive innovations that may put many people, at least temporarily, out of work. From the perspectives of human dignity and personal security, *anxieties* over jobs and status may be more important than actual economic reality. If workers who have safe jobs feel anxious, they will behave as if they are facing economic oblivion and social ostracism. Welfare cannot alleviate such anxiety. But perhaps a well-designed UBI program can.

UBI programs – meaning unconditional, direct, and universally equal payments – offer greater personal security and dignity than means-tested welfare programs because they are unconditional and have no time limits.

Furthermore, by eliminating the bureaucratic layers that test the means of welfare beneficiaries and control and monitor the distribution of welfare, UBI programs would shift funds from administrative intermediaries and put them directly into the hands of beneficiaries. They may make parts of the welfare system redundant – for example, the enactment and monitoring of minimum wage laws. Universal basic income may encourage economic risk taking, entrepreneurship, mobility, prosperity, and professional self-fulfillment, while reducing envy, fear, and resentment, since everybody would receive exactly the same transfer payment. One of the mentioned causes for populism in rich welfare states, competition over scarce welfare resources, may disappear because all would receive the same UBI payment, irrespective of circumstances.

In an era when old political ideologies seem hard pressed to offer viable new policy ideas, UBI is an idea that is cutting through the traditional left–right lines of polarization in interesting ways. Although it is being explored today, mostly on the center-left, for example by democratic presidential candidate Andrew Yang, a generation ago, the push for UBI came from the libertarian-conservative right, counting among its proponents the likes of Milton Friedman, Donald Rumsfeld, Dick Cheney, and – within the context of supporting a carbon tax to pay for UBI – James Baker, Henry Paulson, and George Schultz. Contemporary critics of UBI, such as Hillary Clinton and Joe Biden, retort that such programs would be prohibitively expensive and would require a combination of growth-killing high taxation, government debt, and inflation. Others argue that UBI may create incentives for able workers to become idle rather than take low-paying or otherwise unfulfilling jobs. Consequently, the economy may become less competitive, with more poets and potters and fewer sanitary and social workers. Employers would either have to raise wages beyond those offered in countries without UBI or, when possible, further outsource those jobs. Undoubtedly, in a UBI universe, there would be new risk-taking entrepreneurs, who would generate technological progress, values, and jobs absent from our universe. There would also be able workers who work in our universe but would prefer to live on the public purse in a UBI universe. The question is whether entrepreneurship and self-fulfillment would compensate for the costs of idleness.

Advocates and critics of UBI have theorized and speculated about these questions, and about the virtues and vices of UBI. The Israeli and Polish experience with universal child support strongly indicates that UBI need not bankrupt the state, though it can have unintended consequences on the reproductive habits of the poor. Several pilot programs have been tried recently around the world, and more are planned by public and private institutions. Well-designed and executed pilot programs should generate hard evidence for estimating the costs and benefits of UBI in comparison with those of welfare as we know it. Over time, pilots may measure the extent to which UBI encourages the assumption of economic risks: changing jobs, starting businesses, acquiring education and professional training, becoming geographically mobile, and so on. In the even longer term, it may be possible to measure whether this risk-taking pays off and provides individuals with greater incomes and the state with higher tax revenues to pay for UBI. Less tangibly, pilots may measure how much safer and self-fulfilled – and how much less envious – people feel when they benefit from UBI. It may be possible to discover or refute correlations between increased personal security and decline in populism and increased liberalism.

However, existing and planned pilots display a general misunderstanding of the meaning of UBI. The most famous one, a 2017–2018 pilot in Finland that received extensive press coverage conscripted 2,000 randomly selected *unemployed* Finns to receive €560 per month for two years – an amount comparable to standard Finnish unemployment benefits. If unemployed beneficiaries found employment while enrolled in the program, they continued to receive the €560. Program participants were thus released from an incentive not to work and of the onerous and for some humiliating bureaucratic procedures necessary for receiving unemployment benefits. After two years, the researchers concluded that the experiment had had no effect on rates of employment, though they did find that participants enjoyed improved psychological well-being on various scales by about 10 percent.

This was a UBI pilot in name only. In fact, it was an experiment with a new system for distributing unemployment benefits designed to eliminate disincentives to taking low-wage jobs by limiting the pilot to a random sample of the *unemployed* for a limited time, rather than extending it to all of society, indefinitely. The pilot also did not consider the system of taxation that should evolve to pay for UBI while saving on welfare and administration. Other pilots directed at different disadvantaged sectors of society shared similar weaknesses. At worst, they seem to me like populist publicity stunts marketed as "money for nothing" or "free checks in the mail." Useful UBI pilots must be based on representative samples, divided randomly between experimental and control groups. The "treatment" of the experimental group should be the closest possible simulation of universal basic income. The pilot should measure the effects of UBI on the experimental group by comparing it with the control group and with its own baseline. The groups must be composed of households rather than individuals, because an individual with UBI whose family is not covered will make decisions based on nuisance variables, the total non-UBI income and expenses of the household. The basic income should suffice to live on. It may be based on an index of cost of living, the minimum wage, social security, or a combination of them. UBI should be guaranteed for a lifetime. Elsewhere (Tucker 2019a), I developed in greater detail the design of a scientifically useful UBI pilot. Judgments of the sustainability and affordability of UBI should be deferred until scientific pilots run their course.

If everybody knows from childhood to old age that they will never fall below a socio-economic baseline and that this line is equal for all, existential fear and welfare envy should decrease, if not disappear. Irrespective of transient economic circumstances, it would become difficult for demagogues to manipulate evolutionarily pseudo-extinction perceptions because everybody would know that, irrespective of what happens to them, what they do, how the world economy evolves and so on, they, like everybody else, will always receive the same guaranteed basic income without scarcity or competition of any kind. This would be the political economic version of religious unconditional love.

Dispersing the Anonymous Mob: Tracing Electronic Origins

The internet has recreated the ancient city square in the cloud, filled with mobs and demagogue goading each other on to a frenzy. Mobs are impersonal, unaccountable, irresponsible, and invisible. Their identities are deconstructed and they become an indistinguishable mass of primordial passions, hate, anger, and fear. The introduction of nighttime artificial lights made hiding behind the anonymity of the mob in the centers of towns more difficult. The internet has reconstructed an unlit city without a night watchman, where anonymous gangs and mobs of anonymous bots and trolls can wreak havoc on the polity, minorities, and scapegoats. The city square was also a location where rumors and disinformation could spread quickly and anonymously. Social media can do the same, only faster and more effectively. Disinformation works by appearing to transmit coherent information from the social everywhere and nowhere, while hiding the provenance of the information in a single malevolent source.

The 1927 "Wireless Act" regulated the US radio industry in its infancy (Niklewicz 2017). The survival of liberal democracy requires a comparable Internet Act, as many already agree. In my opinion, the crucial, perhaps painful but necessary, reform would be to curtail net anonymity and introduce mandatory tracing of the origins of signals. The trick is to strike a balance between maintaining freedom of speech and expression for whistleblowers, and even for extremists, and not allowing the disinformers and the mob to hide their identity in order to blur the reliability of what they write. Internet companies should provide information about the provenance of information, the original source of the information. For example, suppose that an innocent user is bombarded by dozens of "news" items that claim that a politician runs a pedophile ring from a pizza parlor in Washington DC, but all the messages also contain information on their provenance, a single source in a nondescript building in a suburb of Moscow.

There are technologies that authenticate provenances, for example for signing legal documents. Other technologies can trace back the route a message took to reach its destination. For example, a message that is being shared and shared again on Facebook or Twitter could come with the route it took from the first sharer to the recipient. Other programs can infer the characteristics of the origin from the intrinsic properties of the message. Finally, human experts may utilize the same methods that philologists, textual critics, historians, and intelligence analysts use to infer textual origins. Facebook was able to trace the sources of Russian disinformation after the fact. They should be able to do it while it is happening, and add to any posting a message about its probable source. There are technical and human solutions for uncovering origins, should there be a political will to use them. The main internet social media companies have the money to pay for such tracing, should the law require them to do so. These companies already have useful technologies, when they limit access of minors to certain websites, authenticate payment, and take down pornography, and malicious notices, e.g. of somebody's death, when the allegedly dead person contacts them to let them know that rumors of their death have been grossly exaggerated, excessively shared, and perhaps unduly "liked."

Anonymity on the internet is not used only by malicious state actors and extremist mobs, but also by dissidents, whistleblowers, and so on, whose rights for free speech without fear should not be compromised. Still, even if anonymity were over-curtailed, it would merely return whistleblowers to where they were in the pre-social media era, a couple of decades ago. A whistleblower used to contact a journalist, a politician, an NGO, or in states that enjoy the rule of law, the police would then investigate and publish the information under their own name. The advantage of this mediation would be that when the information is published it would be fact checked, would not be maliciously damaging, and consumers of the information could rely then on reliable sources, such as serious investigative newspapers.

Historical Education and Commemoration

One of the weirder populist manifestations of fear and distrust of expertise, is the movement of parents who endanger their children and other children by refusing to inoculate them against diseases that in the past killed millions. If only a few children (up to five percent) are not inoculated, it does not matter because, when the vast majority of their friends are inoculated, nobody can infect them. But it should come as no surprise that when a sufficient number of children are not inoculated, diseases that had been eradicated return from the dead to kill. People who were infected and survived acquire natural resistance. Having survived themselves, they are likely to make sure that their children are inoculated. But their grandchildren would be neither survivors nor have parents who are survivors. If neither the state, nor private NGOs, nor wealthy donors have a direct interest in inoculations, historical plagues will return.

Knowledge of history, especially of the nasty parts, is a kind of political inoculation for people lucky enough not to have lived in historically interesting times against the pathologies of Sisyphean politics, the cyclical return of the same failed politics with intervals of two generations. But civic education had all but disappeared from curricula in favor of utilitarian subjects (Mounk 2018, 246–248). Embarrassing national histories have never been popular with education bureaucrats, even when they were still teaching history.

If the purpose of education is exclusively vocational and there are few "jobs" in "history," it is irrational to spend time and public resources on teaching history. Donald Trump himself has said so: he is "not interested" in the past. But neo-illiberalism and populist policies are not exactly cheap; they are much costlier than historical education. The experience of 2016–2017 should serve as a "Sputnik" moment for education in history and the social sciences in the West, as the Soviet launching of Sputnik forced the United States to reexamine American education in STEM subjects and foreign languages. Historical education can work as a circuit breaker for destructive political ideas that were tried and failed miserably. For this reason, civil mass education must include history, and not just that of the glories of the nation and its grievances against its neighbors, but histories of human folly that should not be repeated: e.g., the rise and fall of the Greek polis and the Roman Republic, the French Revolution and its demise, the rise of nationalism and the wars of the twentieth century, the great depression and the rise of Fascism, the Second World War and the Holocaust, the history of racism and colonialism, Communist totalitarianism, the gulags, and the failures of centrally planned economies, and so on. Another outcome would be the overcoming of temporal provincialism, becoming broad minded and more familiar with the diversity of human experiences and existence; in time, that may make students more tolerant.

Historical education can be promoted outside the classroom, through museums and monuments in cityscapes and popular culture. Commemoration is obviously very effective because it raises so much resistance from people who want to restore totalitarianism, neo-Nazis, neo-Communists, and some neo-illiberals. They accuse the victims, the victims' descendants, and their moral allies of being "cry-babies," or, to use their language, of promoting a "lachrymose" historiography. Nazis and Communists killed and tortured millions. So what? Save your tears, let's forget about it, and move on, or even better let's do it all over again. Some of these promoters of historical loss of memory couch their recommendations in the language of post-modern relativism. There is another side to any story, and historiography is just a story. The Holocaust, totalitarianism, the secret police, and the gulags, were all just abstract parts of stories in people's heads. There are other stories and other victims. Nobody mentions how cold it must have been up on the watchtowers above the electrified fences in the winter ... But the guards also have stories to tell. The results should drown the voices of the drowned, and saved in a cacophony of other voices, so nothing would be heard. The best antidote to these attempts to inflict collective dementia on society is to commemorate, remember, and commemorate again, to fight forgetfulness like the dying of the light. For example, a wonderful group of German artists, the "Art Collective Centre for Political Beauty" reacted to a speech by the leading populist neo-illiberal (or simply neo-Nazi) Alternative for Germany (AfD) politician Björn Höcke, where he denounced the Holocaust memorial in Berlin as a "monument of shame in the heart of the capital," by renting the property adjacent to his home, and then legally erecting there a crowd-funded miniature replica of that Holocaust memorial. The artist Philipp Ruch explained the artistic action: Höcke "will now have to deal with the fact that he has neighbors who don't consider the Holocaust memorial a 'monument of shame', but who try to remember what had happened, to prevent it from happening again."

Deliberate attempts to suppress knowledge of the past, prevent commemoration, and facilitate the return of totalitarianism without prejudices against it, are spearheaded by revisionist neo-totalitarian historians. They are hard at work today to use bureaucratic means to impose a narrative saying that there actually never was totalitarianism; that even if there were totalitarianism, it was not so bad; that even if it was bad, the victims consented to the relationship in implicit "social contract"; and that even if they did not consent, they enjoyed it because it provided them with consumer goods, gender equality, and freedom from making choices; these were the classical talking points of Communist propaganda from the 1970s and 1980s. Having encountered a crude attempt to block commemoration of the Holocaust and victims of Communism in the Czech Republic, I personally erected a written bilingual Czech and English "memorial" to the event, where I also discussed this kind of historical revisionism (Tucker 2019b).

Other forms of education for the preemption of populism are sentimental and philosophical. Sentimental education based on Aristotelian rhetoric, philosophy, psychology, and history may train its students to deal with their passions, understand them, and learn how to control them. New sentimental education must teach students how to deal with the augmented technological capacities to manipulate the emotions and use passions (for political goals, to induce consumption, to gamble to encourage addictions, and so on) against users of social media. The anti-passionate virtues, impartiality, restraint, self- control, sangfroid, humor, may be examined and encouraged.

There are significant resources in philosophy and some of the religions for founding identity on morality, freedom, choice, authenticity, life in truth, art, literature, poetry, and so on, that are fairly independent of the vagaries of the markets. If persons can base their sense of identity and dignity on something other than the market, something as simple as being created in the image of God, they should not react to loss of economic status and identity by filling in the void with some constructed tribal nonsense, because there would not be a void there to begin with. A properly educated person in the humanities may be poor, but rarely bored, or in pain from lack of identity. Humane values, decency, honesty, life in truth, artistic sensibility, can substitute for market value. When the unemployed do not ask themselves what their economic value is for other people, but ask what is the intrinsic value of economic activity to them, the answer may be – not much.

Breaking the Glass Barriers to Mobility

Blocked mobility creates a sense of entrapment and hopelessness that many of the victims of recessions feel when they cannot control their lives, despite their efforts. They may then misinterpret their temporary predicament as an extinction event with obvious political repercussions. Social mobility, a sense of control over one's destiny, is the best antidote against such political emotions, and the solidification of a rigid class structure and even more rigid populist xenophobic "class consciousness." The magic of social mobility is that it affects the world view even of people who are not directly affected by it. When people see others like themselves move up the social ladder, their own sense of entrapment and immobility is alleviated. When growth-promoting policies do not work, it is prudent, and in the elite's own enlightened self-interest, to introduce legal and institutional mechanisms to protect and promote social mobility, to open careers to talents, even when it comes at the expense of the less talented or skilled scions and members of the elite. Opening careers to talents should also benefit economic growth over time, when people are matched with positions that fit them the most. When the economy grows, questions of distribution become less urgent. The classical liberal mantras of the nineteenth century were education, social mobility, and opening careers to talents. It was not that easy or simple then, and it has not become easier now.

Historically, removing elites and generating massive social mobility was linear and simple, but violent, difficult, and counterproductive. Massive social force was used to remove entrenched elites in revolutions and civil wars. But the intended and unintended consequences of such linear class warfare often proved the cure worse than the disease, if not a worse disease to begin with. The totalitarian terrors of the French and Bolshevik revolutions and Mao's Cultural Revolution indeed eliminated elites and created continuous mobility. But they did so by first killing off the old elites, then killing off their replacements, and so on, until the revolution consumed itself and a new class structure became stable and permanent; and worse than the old class structure because it had one party-state hierarchy, rather than multiple competing ones, and too many people died in the process. The basic paradox of linear class replacement is that, in order to remove by brute force a powerful entrenched elite, the state must construct an even more powerful elite, most notably of the secret police, that it is even more difficult to remove, and so on.

A more liberal way to increase mobility is by finding non-linear inflection points that can increase mobility without guillotines and gulags; for example by removing social barriers, obstacles, or bottlenecks that the elite put on the path to mobility.

In the post-totalitarian world, the entrenched elite descends from the old totalitarian elite, since there was a political but no social revolution. While the late totalitarian elite relinquished direct control over politics, it maintained control of the commanding heights of the economy and the newly independent nominally liberal state institutions. They should have been separated from capital, the scarcest resource following Communism. This could have been done by quickly selling the banking and insurance monopolies to foreign banks and distributing the proceeds among all the citizens. The sizes of universities should have grown exponentially and quickly, by importing university teachers to generate quickly the missing educated elites that could have replaced the totalitarian elites in the judiciary, law enforcement, and the governing heights of the economy. At the very beginning of the transitions, governments chose to keep those old elites in power, rather than bring in foreigners to do the job in the absence of indigenous elites. (In the Baltic states, they did accept returning immigrant co-nationals to replace the Russian elites; perhaps consequently they have weaker populist neo-illiberal movements in comparison with the countries that rejected former emigres.)

Heavily regulated labor markets could have been *deregulated* by legislation to facilitate mobility. For example, the Central European model of long-term employment in a single institution, from apprenticeship to seniority subjects promotion to patronage, in a single career path. Judges, an obviously significant example, must start as clerks to judges, and then slowly advance. They usually do not work as independent lawyers. Such arrangements make it difficult to inject new blood across social hierarchies. (Tucker 2015, 66–70)

To make room at the top, post-totalitarian governments could have used more extensive and stringent rules of lustration, the exclusion of secret police officers and agents from the higher echelons of government and other institutions. Their replacement would have generated mobility. The judiciary and adjacent legal professions should have been entirely replaced and overhauled by rapid expansion of law schools and appointments to the judiciary of newly minted lawyers. Populist parties finally recently replaced judges and other officials, but they were replaced with a *new class* of non-meritocratic politically dependent and loyal cadre of the neo-illiberal parties. Neo-illiberals today obey Robert Michels' iron law of the oligarchy, like everybody else, to create Djilas' new class. (The Yugoslav Communist Djilas argued famously that the Communists did not eliminate class structure but created a new bureaucratic upper class of functionaries.) Whenever and however neo-illiberalism comes to an end, if it is replaced by liberal democrats, they will have to purge the judiciary and other institutions again; only this time of incompetent neo-illiberals, rather than totalitarians, and open careers to talents, rather than to political loyalists, among other reasons to generate social mobility.

Some of the post-Communist populist resentment directed against the European Union is displaced resentment, scapegoating, for lack of mobility within the European Union. The promise of the post-1989 revolutions and the ascension to the European Union was a convergence with Western Europe. Czechs, Slovaks, and Hungarians were once in the Austro-Hungarian Empire. There was no reason for them, apart from Communism, not to be as prosperous as their neighbors in Austria. This promise was fulfilled insufficiently. Post-Communist countries have never been in a better social and economic shape. They experienced massive absolute mobility as a result of economic liberalization, membership of the European Union, and trade, especially with Germany. However, the workers who build German cars want now to be paid like German workers. They measure themselves, not in comparison with their younger selves, but in comparison with their West European peers. They want to have relative mobility in their foreign-owned companies and in Europe in general. Here, the European Union encounters a problem in its very design. It is a union of independent nation-states with regulated free trade and freedom of movement, but it is not a United States of Europe. Nations erect barriers to the social mobility of other Europeans. Sure, East Europeans can pick asparagus and do other jobs that Germans do not. They earn more working for German international companies in their own countries. But their road to the German middle and upper classes is blocked. There are no Czechs or Hungarians on the corporate boards of the companies that employ them, hardly any professors in German universities, and so on. West European nation-states block mobility by over-regulation of labor markets and by spontaneous xenophobia, not considering "foreigners" for middle and upper-class jobs. The efforts of the European Union in this respect are laudable, though they have been undermined by European nation-states. If Europe is united and equal, Europeans should enjoy mobility everywhere.

The elites of traditional liberal democracies that turned neo-illiberal do not originate in a totalitarian party-state. But, like their post-Communist peers, they still protect themselves from downward mobility during recessions by blocking mobility. The growing awareness that there is a serious social problem with mobility in the United States and other countries with strong populist and neo-illiberal movements has led to many useful suggestions. For example, to retool affirmative action, as in the UK, to be based on class (Reeves 2017).

Rather than reiterate and discuss these excellent proposals, I want to emphasize the link between facilitation of mobility and preemption of populist neo-illiberal democracy. Then I add a longer discussion of my ideas for overcoming one of the main barriers to mobility in the United States and a few other countries, though by no means all neo-illiberal democracies, which is the misuse of educational institutions for class construction and hoarding of opportunities.

Many authors noted that excessive regulations construct barriers to competition that exclude socially and economically mobile newcomers. Commercial regulations preclude the entrance of new firms to markets and create oligopolies of old firms. Formal and informal professional regulations prevent new professionals from joining established elites. Zoning regulations keep out migrants from prosperous areas where they may find work and become socially mobile and politically liberal. All reduce competition for elites at the cost of blocking the mobility of others. The interesting aspect of this manifestation of what I called elite populism is that its victims, the ones whose mobility is blocked, turn around and apply similar measures to those still socially lower than them. They try to keep international migrants from poor countries from settling, working, and opening businesses where they live, just as the elites do to them with greater implicit subtlety. Elite populism begets popular populism.

In many liberal democratic countries, and some that are not, educational institutions are misused for the maintenance, defense, formation, selling, and marketing of exclusionary social class. Education magnifies exponentially preexisting inequality (Fishkin 2014, 205–212; Reeves 2017, 55–56). Educational certificates and social networks associated with them are the glass floors of the elite penthouse. Since, in addition to constructing and selling class, educational institutions may also educate, evaluate, assess, and certify, conduct original research, publish it in scientific journals and popular venues, they also sell meritocratic legitimization of the class structure. "Educated people mistake their tribalism for superior wisdom" (Runciman 2018, 164).

At the center of the enigma of class and education there are mysteries, the secret criteria for *admission* and *certification of graduation*. Fishkin called this class-based scheme "diabolical." Fishkin described the American higher education system as designed to maximize the effects of class and wealth by limiting social status and employment opportunities to students who can afford to pay for many years for the most expensive education. Cost-sensitive parents are tempted to send their scions to less prestigious but cheaper institutions of higher education, which would severely limit their employment opportunities. "A diabolical planner attempting to create an opportunity structure with as severe a class bottleneck as possible would ... arrange even the four-year colleges in a status hierarchy and replace need-based financial aid with merit aid aimed at inducing students to attend a college where they stand out as an especially strong applicant – which is to say, a college just a bit lower in the status hierarchy than the one they might have chosen to attend if money were no object. Merit aid thus pulls students whose families are more price sensitive downward in the college status hierarchy, freeing up spots above so that children from less price-sensitive (and generally wealthier) families can move up" (Fishkin 2014, 207–208). Unpaid internships further limit mobility to those with contacts to obtain them and with funds to be able to provide for themselves while gaining experience, which again discriminates against those who must take paid internships. While Fishkin talked of higher education, similar analysis *mutandis mutatis* holds for earlier stages of education.

Fishkin's "diabolical scheme" is a case of what I called elite populism. Eventually, it is self-destructive because it generates too much resentment channeled also into popular populism. It also keeps out too many talented people who would use their brains to bring it down, while keeping in too many untalented scions of the elite who would not know how to contend with their intellectual superiors. An orderly, rather than revolutionary, opening of the elites to poorer children and students from the lower classes would be in everybody's enlightened interest, but the history of elite populism from the Greeks through the Romans, to the French and Russian nobilities, does not provide a basis for optimism. Elite populists eventually get it, but often that happens only when the guillotine hits them – too late.

Discrimination in favor of old elites is now entirely explicit only in the United States, where schools and universities that sell entrance to the elite discriminate against applicants whose parents or other relatives did not graduate from the same schools and universities and did not donate to them; and, in the case of publicly financed state or local schools, against children who live outside a district to begin with and, secondly, outside a radius of busing. For example, a wealthy suburb of Boston will have private-independent schools that would discriminate against the children of parents who did not study there, against parents not wealthy enough to pay, and public-municipal schools that would discriminate against the children of parents who live in poorer districts and though they bus in some children from poorer neighborhoods in and around Boston, they obviously cannot bus in children from the deep South.

A mystery lingers in estimating the exact numbers of potential students who would have enjoyed upper mobility had they not been discriminated against. This class repro-duction system exacts external costs from society, not just in blocking the mobility of highly talented students whose sole fault is their parents' social class, but in gener-ating popular resentment against "rigged" class structure, isolated elites, and biased expertise. It also prevents not so talented children of rich people from occupying social roles that are appropriate to their merit and where they would not do much damage to society. Otherwise, the elite, through elite universities, impose exorbitant external costs on society. For example, the Trump dynasty and its associates, even members who are clearly fluent in no more than half a language and ignorant about history and politics, received their entry pass to the American elite and to affecting other people's lives from elite private schools and universities, for which their families paid well above the tuition asking price. Even suppose that those institu-tions used the donations they received from those families to educate tenfold poor and deserving kids, are their improved prospects worth what the undeserving children of the rich have been putting the world through?!

In other countries, in continental Europe, where private education is illegal or cannot compete with free public education, such pro-elite *overt* discrimination is impos-sible. Nevertheless, there is substantial class continuity across generations. Upper-class people with good degrees are better at navigating the state educational bureaucratic system and preparing their scions for competing in it than outsiders.

The simplest linear policy remedy may be simply to eliminate by law all elite education. Even if the state attempts to enforce explicit and transparent meritocratic admission and graduation requirements, elites find ways to circumvent them and reuse elite institutions for class reproduction. For example, The French *École Nationale d'administration* (ENA) was created as a highly selective meritocratic institute of higher learning by de Gaulle in 1945 to train high civil servants to eliminate prewar bureaucratic patronage and incompetence that contributed to France's defeat in the war. But the French upper classes found ways to game the system and, instead of devoting their university years to studying, ENA students spent their time networking to position for elite jobs. President Macron understood it because he himself is an ENA alumnus. So he closed down the institution.

The French Revolution went furthest and abolished higher education altogether. Eliminating all higher education is impossible in modern economies. Napoleon was forced to found the present French higher education system because he needed educated bureaucrats, engineers, and soldiers. Revolutionary Communist regimes undertook to generate radical social mobility without shutting down universities by barring higher education from all but the children of the working classes. The teachers' class background also weighed in on their employment retention prospects. The definitions of "working class" could be flexible though. But the result was fairly backward and small higher education systems. Educational abolition is not a viable option.

It is possible to provide uniform education to all in state schools and mega-universities that teach every-thing to everybody for free, as is the case in some continental European countries. Such an extreme linear egalitarian solution, however, may make the problem of class reproduction without mobility more severe and impose other externalities on society. Elites are ingenious when it comes to protecting their families. For example, in England, when many selective state-financed high schools, "grammar schools," were closed down and gave way to egalitarian comprehensives, they closed down a route of upper mobility for talented middle-class and working-class children. The elite continued to send its scions to private schools, which educate only seven percent of British children. But, since the abolition of grammar schools, the wealthier children have not had to compete against so many certified meritocratic children of lower classes. If elite private education is abolished in one country, its elite can move its children to another, to boarding schools in Switzerland or England, colleges and universities in the United States and so on.

Other drawbacks of radical elite education abolition are external to the issue of mobility. Not all students are the same. So, uniform education cannot fit all equally well. Some diversity is useful. Uniform, centrally managed public education has not been an overwhelming success, for the general reasons that central planning fails, bureaucrats do not have the information to allocate resources efficiently. State institutions can become self-serving for their employees, who block change and provide poor service. Financial dependence on the state can limit the number of students and impoverish universities at best, and facilitate illiberalism at worst, as employees of Hungarian universities know too well. These drawbacks explain why the class-obsessed warts-and-all American higher education system is still so dominant and desirable in the global market for education and research. In order not to throw the students out along with the academic mobility blocking bath waters, educational institutions should continue to compete over offering the best education and engaging in the best research, without unqualified bureaucrats telling them what and how to teach, what to write, and about what to conduct research (Tucker 2015, 190–203).

Preempting populism of the upper and lower classes requires, then, legal assistance for independent educational institutions, in order for them to keep competing, by offering the best education and conducting the best research, *while exiting the market for class membership and access to social networking.* One simple and cheap, but limited, solution may be the legal prohibition of educational incest. The admission of children to the schools their parents attended could be made as illegal as marrying them. But elites could adjust to such a regulation by generating informal or even formal agreements to exchange the children of alumni between elite exclusionary schools. Such regulation would surely create more hybridity *within* the elite, and perhaps some limited, better than at present, mobility from without. But this is surely not enough.

A more radical solution of wider scope, which I would like to develop is to neutralize the class advantage that schools and universities confer on their graduates by connecting their admission rates to their class advantage: the greater is the advantage, the higher should be the admission rate. It could work like this: A statistical agency would measure the effect each school and university has on the class membership of its alumni; for example, by preparing a list of the elite positions in a profession (because they pay the most, or are the most prestigious, or are most in demand and so on). The statistical office can then match the people on that list (or a statistical sample of them) with the schools they attended. Suppose they discover that 50 percent of those positions, like those on the American Supreme Court, are filled by the alumni of a single university, meaning attending that university is a prerequisite for membership in 50 percent of elite positions. 50 percent should then become the admission rate to that university. Such compulsory admission rate would neutralize the effect of admission on class. The law would then force the university to increase its admission rate to 50 percent.

Elite schools and universities would then be forced to act like other successful brand name firms, which sell excellent products and want to maximize profit: increase production, or franchise. Quality-cars makers open a dealership in every major town, as do hotel chains and Starbucks coffee shops. Why not brand name schools and universities that sell excellent education?! With admission policies that neutralize class, it would not matter if schools and universities were to admit legacy students, the children of donors and so on. Good schools and universities may have hundreds of thousands or millions of students, and have campuses around the world, so they would benefit from the economies of scale. Increased supply should increase profits while reducing costs and prices/tuition fees. Competition may then bankrupt uncompetitive schools and universities, in the usual process of creative destruction that generates progress.

Schools and universities should continue to sell excellent education, and quite possibly absolute mobility (in relation to parents) but no social class advantage. According to this rule, the more an institution is effective in blocking the mobility of graduates of its competitors, the less selective it should become and vice versa. New or small boutique schools or universities with no, or small, representation in the elite would be able to be as selective as they wish and have well-defined niches to prosper in, from which they could embark to disrupt the market. Once they are successful enough to plug graduates into the elite, they will have to become less selective, and so on. In this way, the education market would be forced to emulate the working of normal markets for services, as distinct from markets for social class. The market for class (like club membership or art and high-end fashion markets) may maximize profits by severely limiting supply. Markets for services maximize profits by creating economies of scale, becoming more efficient to reduce price, and increasing supply to expand to new markets directly or by franchise.

Note that this system does not guarantee graduation. Schools and universities would be forced to admit, but not to graduate. They may maintain or rather introduce strict graduation criteria. It is necessary then to force schools and universities to introduce meritocratic graduation criteria, so they do not admit millions but graduate the same few thousand children of the elite. The best way to achieve that, while opening even more channels for social mobility, is by *the institutional separation of education from evaluation.* Universities should continue to do what they do best, educate and conduct research, and schools should teach and educate. But the evaluation of the results should be undertaken by separate independent institutions. Currently, educational institutes are under irresistible pressures to graduate their students and inflate their grades, by paying parents, state bureaucrats, and independent institutions that construct academic hierarchies, partly on the basis of graduation rates. This leads to a good deal of rigging of the evaluation process, not to mention fraud when teachers forge the exams of their students or otherwise inflate their grades (Tucker 2015, 178–203; Muller 2018). This can be preempted by institutionally distinguishing education from evaluation.

Some professional associations, in law and medicine for example, conduct their own certification processes. Yet, their results are reported as pass or fail, e.g. medical doctors become "board certified," and lawyers are admitted to the bar, or not. But suppose certifying exams are introduced in most fields, run by competing independent professional or state sponsored associations, and *the exact grades examinees receive, not just if they passed or failed, can be reported to potential employers, research grant funders* or made public. This would open another avenue for mobility to people irrespective of the institutions they graduated from, *even if they did not graduate from any school.* In some countries with high-school exams, such external exams already exist for high-school certificate. The ultimate literary hero of social mobility, Lewis Eliot, the protagonist of C. P. Snow's *Strangers and Brothers* never went to university, but studied by himself to pass the exams to become a barrister and then became a Cambridge don. Such a hundred-year-old story would be entirely surreal today. But the world would benefit from many more Lewis Eliots, if for no other reason than that people who experience such mobility are not likely to become populist neo-illiberals, even though, toward the end of his life, Eliot did vote Conservative for the first time.

Separating evaluation and certification from institutional education would release educational institutions from spending resources on gaming the certification and assessment process. Degrees and their brand names should become less significant. Students should then go to schools and universities to actually study and conduct research. Students may study at several good institutions with different outstanding teachers, as was normal in previous centuries, when education was exclusively about *education*. After studying with the best, they may take an exam when they feel ready to enter the working world, with or without bothering to obtain a university degree in addition to the certified professional diploma.

Schools and universities could still use the oldest and most lethal weapon in class warfare, raise tuition fees. A university may admit a million students, but if it charges a million dollars in tuition, so its students' dormitories would double as five-star resorts with room service, it will keep all but the richest students out. I suspect this is not a real problem because, had this been a viable business model, somebody in America would have tried it by now (and some have already tried similar models, arguing that universities are like Vodka brands, they are all the same product; the difference is in the marketing and the price tags). If elites use blunt financial weapons against the lower classes they will dispose of all the mystery, magic, and wizardry of education and the elaborate meritocratic façade would crumble to dust. They would have to admit they are social clubs and not institutions of learning.

"Hogwarts" will expose itself as mere Mar-a-Lago. By raising tuition, they would lower their market value, and then would have no customers. My proposed regulations should facilitate competition. New schools and universities should be able to enter the market and offer better education for lower prices and have unconstrained admission policies because, as new institutions, they will have no alumni in the elite. States can also do what they already do now: cap tuition fees, give tuition coupons, guarantee loans, and so on while maintaining the independence of institutions. Still, competition between universities and the institutional separation of evaluation and certification from education should do most of the work.

Of course, as critics of my ideas will point out, there would be an escalating arms race between the regulations and the ingenuity of smart and successful parents who love their children. The smarter the regulations get, the more the clever parents will look for ways to circumvent them. For example, the excellent American meritocratic concept of universal university exams administered by an independent university board led to unintended consequences: An industry that prepares students with time and money for these exams, which are still marketed mythically as preparation-proof, though every insider knows it is a bluff; with enough time and money it is possible to turn a mediocre student into an excellent examinee. An even more sinister, partly illegal, industry of admission councilors sells proprietary methods for gaming the admission system. But the fact that thieves become ever more sophisticated is no reason for the police to give up. Regulations and their enforcement would have to keep up the arms race with the parents indefinitely.

A final concern may be that even if regulations like the ones I outlined, and other similar ones, are successful in approaching a meritocratic ideal and enable mobility, there will still be intergenerational class continuities for other reasons, such as genetic inheritance. Some amateur geneticists think that smart or otherwise talented parents beget similar children who, in a meritocratic universe, will occupy similar social positions to those of their parents and block the aspirations of less talented people, who would then resent them and succumb to populist temptations. These assumptions about genetics are scientifically doubtful. The kind of cognitive skills that have become useful in advanced economies, for example, the manipulation of symbolic data, were entirely useless for virtually all of evolutionary history. Consequently, we would expect thousands of genes and environmental factors to be involved in developing many different skills. The result of so many factors would be fairly even, a random distribution of unequal innate skills in large populations, which get reshuffled each generation. In this respect, the genetics of cognitive skills is probably closer to that of sexual orientation than to that of eye color. This is pretty much what we see. There are more talented Chinese and Indians than talented members of other single ethnic groups because there are more Chinese and Indians in the world. There are also more untalented Chinese and Indians. The sorting of mates according to class, which should generate unequal genetically based classes, was practiced by European and other inherited nobilities for hundreds of years. The results were genetically debilitating mutations and sterility, not master races. In-breeding is not a successful strategy for biological or social survival.

There are cultural and other environmental contexts that favor or disfavor mobility. But cultures are affected by social contexts. People trapped in their class will not encourage their children to study hard because it would constitute an investment without a possible return. But when social circumstances change, cultures adapt. For example, the academic successes of Ashkenazi Jews have led some speculative biologists and amateur geneticists to suggest genes are involved. It is easy to forget that during the mass migration of Jews from Eastern Europe to the United States in the late nineteenth century, they were known mostly for their excellence in boxing. For much of the eighteenth century, they were associated in Central Europe with the rag trade in second-hand clothes. Then, admission to universities became possible and Ashkenazi Jews who, indeed, had always had higher rates of literacy than class-comparable gentiles, for cultural reasons took advantage of the opportunity, and the cultural stereotypes followed. If this book has not convinced you of it already, take it from an insider: with all due respect to those Ashkenazi Jews who won 20 percent of the Nobel Prizes, there are also plenty of dull Ashkenazi Jews out there.

Liberalism promised a universal solution to the ancient problems of human flourishing in society. This universal promise is its strength and weakness. The universal promise is appealing to all. Its universality makes it a particularly dangerous ideology for authoritarians and illiberals. It has been so since the seventeenth century. However, exactly because liberalism makes a universal promise, when liberals renege on their promise and create barriers to universal meritocracy, they generate disappointment, disillusionment, and resentment. It is impossible to run the political equivalent of a universal religion like an exclusive social club, open only to those who were born into it or are able to pay exorbitant admission prices. Liberalism cannot be an expensive luxury. Exclusion creates the perception of hypocrisy. It is hypocritical to pay homage to universal rights, personal autonomy, and meritocracy, and then block mobility, and use the quintessential enlightenment liberal institutions of education for this purpose. Liberals discredit liberalism's universal promise when they practice elite populism for the short-term protection of their social class. When privileged liberal elites condescend, they add insult to injury. Liberalism must save itself by constructing institutions that prevent liberals from betraying their creed because they love their families more than they care for the long-term survival of their civilization.

The promise of the enlightenment, nineteenth-century liberalism and twentieth-century progressivism was of human flourishing, and absolute and relative mobility through education. A new liberal restoration will need to reimagine this dream of secular, social, and cultural salvation through education. The centuries-old promise of enlightenment rationalism and liberal progressivism must be kept. Of course, this is not a panacea or an attempt at a panacea for social injustice. I argued that neo-illiberal populism is fed by absence of mobility for the lower middle and middle classes. These neo-illiberal populists are not concerned with equality or welfare, because they believe they serve other people. I propose, then, measures for unblocking social and geographic mobility.

Geographic Mobility

Much ink has been spilled over the alleged split between a global cosmopolitan elite of multi-lingual urbanites, who float in their professional yachts on the surface of the high seas of the global economy, and the poor souls who are rooted in the harsh and barren soil of their native obsolescence and cannot take advantage of globalization. This interpretation leaves out the economic fact that many more poor people are the greatest beneficiaries of globalization, migrants of all sorts from the poor unskilled, through students, to professionals, and entrepreneurs, and the people they employ. Formerly poor people who live in emerging economies that supply advanced economies with cheap goods, services, and migrant labor are also the beneficiaries of globalization. This large population is ignored because, unlike the numerically much smaller resentful populists in the first world, they are not dangerous to the liberal elites who decide what is dangerous and whose suffering counts. The lower classes of advanced industrial economies have benefitted from the cheap goods that flow from developing countries, or are made by immigrants. But they prefer to forget or not notice it. For example, for the first time in history even the poorest Europeans and Americans no longer walk barefoot, or dress in rags, because clothes and shoes have become so cheap.

There is vast literature from economics and the social sciences that examines and proves the overwhelming economic, political, and cultural advantages of migration. A world with open borders is likely to double global GDP and generate the strongest economic boom in human history (cf. Guest 2011 and the special report Guest edited for the *Economist* on migration, November 16, 2019). The retort of commentators who accept these data is that the benefits are not spread equally to all people at all times in all regions. This is undoubtedly true. However, it is often overlooked that states and their policies, rather than impersonal economic forces unleashed by globalization, contribute to the divide between elites that benefit from globalization and populists who do not. State regulations and policies about globalization discriminate in particular against two groups that are sometimes associated with populism and neo-illiberalism but could have benefitted from globalization: Retirees and the unemployed.

Retirees on fixed state pensions are often challenged by the high cost of living. They can enjoy a considerably higher standard of living if they move from the first world to countries with considerably lower costs of living, as indeed some retirees do. But some government policies that link their benefits, most notably health insurance, with where they live, keep retirees from moving to inexpensive sunny countries and flourish in the globalized village. If governments began providing medical insurance for retirees abroad, and facilitated retiree mobility with inter-national agreements, a global exchange of populations would benefit both sides. The planes that would bring retirees to places like Mexico, could bring back young labor to places like Chicago, where the migrants would pay for the social security transfer payments to the retirees through taxation. The retirees would then take it with them back to Mexico. Another service that pensioners would appreciate receiving from their states while living globally is security. Sometimes rightly and sometimes wrongly, pensioners believe they may have a higher chance of suffering from crime in cheaper countries. Already now there are agreements between states that allow foreign police forces to protect and regulate their compatriots abroad. For example, British police can accompany British football fans abroad. Czech police regulate in the summer Croatian beaches that are popular with Czech tourists. Military police supervise soldiers stationed in foreign military bases, and also when they are off base. States can send some policemen with retirees to regulate and serve expatriate communities. Eliminating these barriers would replicate the successes of Florida and the Iberian Peninsula as retiree destinations, but on a grander global scale with much greater savings for global retirees.

Similarly, the unemployed who cannot find work are forced to continue to reside within a state or sovereign boundaries in order to receive unemployment benefits. This makes no long-term sense. If somebody cannot find employment where they live within a reasonable timeframe, they should be allowed to take their unemployment benefits anywhere else, either to where they may have a better chance to find work, or to where those benefits have the highest purchasing power.

Some pensioners and long-term unemployed may still resent elites and blocked mobility and their populist passions may still be present. But over time, in a beachside community in countries like Mexico, Costa Rica, or Thailand, they may relax. The passions would subside. The rat race half a world away may recede into irrelevance. As was the case with other migrations, a successful trickle may become a torrent, and a stream a river. Disaffected populist illiberals may discover the joys of globalization and simply stop caring, tune in and drop out as boomer generation retirees may have said when they were great, and now again. The global economic-political system may reach in this way a kind of stable equilibrium beneficial to all.

Free trade without free movement and labor mobility generates disequilibria. The solution is not to limit free trade, but link free trade to free mobility, so the disequilibria generated by trade may be balanced by the movements of people. Workers from the first world should be allowed to work abroad legally, and even chase their jobs there if they are outsourced, especially in countries that have free trading agreements with each other, and in developing countries that are the sources of immigration to the first world. For example, if China wants to export to the United States, and Mexico send migrant workers there, Americans should be allowed to settle in China and Mexico, work, open businesses and so on. To facilitate this type of moving, states should link free trade agreement to agreements on free access to labor markets.

Is this an "outlandish" proposal, as one sympathetic reader of this book put it? All these exit options for workers and entrepreneurs, retirees and welfare beneficiaries would be entirely voluntary. They would not make anybody's life worse than they are now, but they may help many people who are locked out of globalization at present appreciate and share in its benefits.

Historically, before the invention of borders to limit immigration around the turn of the twentieth century, Europeans and their descendants chased opportunities, capital and trade. They used "exist" options to improve their lives. For this reason, the nineteenth century offered Europeans mobility and growth that accompanied liberalization and democratization, the classical "Whiggish" pace of linear progress that the twentieth century, with its recessions and wars, missed. Unfortunately, much of this was accompanied by occupation and imperialism, and even genocide, when West Europeans set out to occupy the globe. Now, after five hundred years, migration flows have finally reversed to become truly globalized. Since most migrants are not Europeans, they by and large accept the laws of the countries they migrate to, do not impose or occupy, but seek voluntary exchanges of labor and goods. There is a tiny Moslem minority that does not accept the laws of man, but by and large Europeans are projecting their own past imperialisms on very different types of migrants who are not imperialistic. A further flow of migrants from the North to the South may make economic sense and spread the benefits of globalization to some Northerners who are locked out of it at present.

Some argued in the wake of the coronavirus pandemic that it demonstrated the dark side of globalization. Closed borders may make little economic or cultural sense, but they allegedly prevent the spreading of diseases. Still, there is no correlation between immigration, migration, and the spread of diseases. The coronavirus spread from Wuhan in inner China, not from any of the traditional sources of immigration or refugees in the Middle East, Afghanistan, or Latin America. Effective isolation of infected region in the United States does not include the border with Mexico, but regions within the United States.

Neither the problem of pandemics nor its most effective solutions fit national borders or nation-states. Pandemics emerged in a particular region and, if its quarantine is the solution, it does not coincide with political borders. Isolation may be regional or based on social networks of physical interaction, not national. Medical authorities need to quarantine regions and individuals who were exposed, not countries or nation-states. National borders actually get in the way of demarcating the relevant social and geographical areas for quarantine, and the optimization of the distribution of medical supplies. When each nation-state hoards types of medical equipment, whether they are necessary or not, they may prevent their optimal allocation to where they are most needed. Finally, the real solution for pandemics is scientific–pharmaceutical and hence global. This solution requires cooperation across borders, internationally, to discover, develop, and produce medicines and vaccines, and be ready to preempt the next unexpected emergence of a pandemic, hopefully not for another hundred years.

Strengthening Liberal Institutions

Odysseus famously ordered his sailors to bind him to the ship's mast before he heard the Sirens sing because he knew he would not be able to control his passions once he heard them. Jon Elster suggested that constitutions resemble Odysseus' bounds; the state binds itself when it is sober but can foresee the possibility of intoxication by passions. For example, the deflationary effects of tightening credit in the 1930s and inflationary effects of loosening monetary policies under populist governments in the 1970s led to the construction of politically and institutionally independent central banks that set interest rates. Zakaria (2003, 242) advocated the creation and expansion of liberal technocratic institutions, isolated and independent of democratic and potentially populist pressures. He hailed the European Union, which he described as "the only anti-protectionist free market agent in a continent resistant to change and deregulation." But Zakaria (2003) also noted that populist and even not so populist politicians use liberal institution as scapegoats for unpopular though rational complex policies for which they do not want to take responsibility. Liberal institutions that are isolated from politics cannot retaliate, so they are ideal whipping boys. Some of the populist hostility to the European Union resulted from such scapegoating. The classical retort is that we need more democracy rather than less and democratic neo-illiberal populists will learn from their mistakes over time, if they remember them and there is still a democracy in the end. The nature of the passions is that they ebb and flow and when they flow, they flood reason and drown interests. In populist cultures, for example in some Latin American societies, cycles of populism follow the passions, ecstasy, disillusionment, disappointment, self-destruction, sobriety, and again the passions. Democracy cannot be held hostage to passions. Liberal institutions must constrain the passions to allow democracy to function and avoid self-destruction.

As much as tightening credit in a recession is a destructive yet intuitive emotional response, restrictions on trade and labor mobility – protectionism and immigration restrictions – are instinctive passionate populist responses to recessions that deepen and prolong them, and then metastasize them globally. An institutional solution to this problem may be similar, the founding of constitutionally independent boards to protect the global economy from self-destructive political passions. The framework of an organization like the World Trade Organization could serve as a basis for international agreements for constituting such a board for international trade. Independent immigration boards composed of impartial economists, urbanists, artists, and so on can be tasked with specifying optimal levels of migration for economic, urban, and cultural growth.

Even better would be to depoliticize migration entirely, as was the case until the late nineteenth century. Until fairly recently in human history, immigration was not politicized. There were no immigration restrictions, and people accepted it as they did any number of natural phenomena. Immigrants were, however, mistreated, discriminated against, or exploited, because they were usually weaker and without a local support network. The Bible for example, repeatedly warns against mistreating the three weakest groups in society, widows, orphans, and immigrants (residents *gerim* is the literal term). It reminds the readers repeatedly that the people of Israel were immigrants in Egypt and that Abraham was an immigrant from Haran. The patriarch Isaac is just about the only person of note in *Genesis* who was not a migrant, and maybe because of that he did not run away when his dad tried to kill him.

Immigration restrictions emerged in tandem with the imposition of equal civil rights. Once second-class citizenship was taken off the table as a legal option, political society was left with a bivalent choice between allowing immigrants to remain as full and equal citizens, and keeping them out of sovereign nation-states. It is no surprise that the first immigration restrictions, against Chinese family unification and migration in America, emerged after the Civil War abolished slavery and established equal citizenship, at least in legal theory. Intermediary schemes of "guest laborers," euphemistic labels for second-class residents, since the Second World War failed because they amounted to reintroducing second-class citizenship and hence created resentment. Laborers legitimately want either to become full and equal citizens, buy homes, invest, subscribe to magazines, or go somewhere else; nobody wants to be a second-class resident.

Athenian citizens voted on the results of trials, and elected their military generals. This led to injustices and military defeats. Today, practically nobody feels they do not have full exercise of their right to democratic self-determination because they cannot vote on verdicts and on the leadership of the military. Most people would find it difficult to imagine it otherwise. Within a generation or two, there will be societies where everybody has always lived in societies where same-sex couples could be married. Few would imagine that it could be any business of the democratic state to decide by a vote who can or cannot marry whom. Then it will become socially entrenched and a social norm. Likewise, there may come a time when people would accept that it is no business of the state to tell people with whom they can and cannot trade, or whom they are allowed to employ or work for, and it will also become again an entrenched norm.

Arguably, if international trade and immigration are depoliticized, politics, democratic choice, self-determination, and sovereignty would diminish. Still, a basic list of democratic sovereign decisions that have nothing to do with the movements of people and goods would include decisions on war or peace, how much the state would tax and how, how the state would spend taxes, criminal and civil laws, and state regulations of the environment. The ordinary choices in the economic libertarian versus socialist and social liberal versus conservative continuums would still be offered in all their varieties and nuances. Only some populist political passions will be off the political menu, much like monarchist politics in Austria, anti-Semitic politics in Germany, and theocratic politics in France. Some Austrian monarchists, German anti-Semites, and French theocratic parties may complain that democracy in their countries is fake because they are prohibited from running in elections, so citizens are allowed to choose between liberal democratic options, rather than vote for a monarchy, a Nazi dictatorship, or a theocracy. I beg to differ. Austria, Germany, and France had good reason to be wary of particular types of political passions that almost destroyed those countries. To protect their common interests, they introduced constitutions that took off the democratic menu the most destructive options, much like Europeans took Absinth off their drinking menus around the turn of the previous century.

Human beings have always moved from places that were bad for them to places where they hoped to be better off; most notably to places where they expected to be more secure, free, and prosperous. American prosperity is due to a large extent to the fact that many Americans have been moving around a big and diverse continent with different opportunities. One of the symptoms of the current economic problems of the United States is that Americans move at about half the rate they used to in the 1950s. Among the main explanations are that American estate agents currently take about six percent of the value of bought and sold houses, which creates a disincentive for moving. Zoning and other restrictions on construction keep the prices of housing in the economically vibrant parts of the country too high. For example, California can be an expensive place to live. Some Californians therefore move up the pacific coast to Oregon, and Washington State, or East to Nevada and even Idaho. Locals do not always welcome the Californians. Prague in the early 1990s attracted graduates of the University of California in Santa Barbara. So, other expatriates claimed not to want to be "Santa Barbarized." But none of the above was a political issue. A couple of generations ago, an environmental disaster in Oklahoma drove many "Okie" farmers to settle in California. Their culture and manners were stranger to Californians than those of contemporary Mexicans to Texans, or of Irish to residents of Boston, or of Israelis to New Yorkers; yet it did not become a political issue.

Democratic Election Systems

Different democratic electoral systems can generate entirely different results from the same distributions of votes. Majoritarian, or first past the post, electoral systems facilitate neo-illiberalism when the illiberal party is in the minority, but faces fragmented opposition, as in Hungary and Poland; or when the system is gerrymandered or otherwise unrepresentative, as in some US elections, including the state electors' system of voting for president, which does not consider sizes of majorities in states. It is striking that of all of the neo-illiberal populists, the only one actually to win a majority of the votes was Hungary's Fidesz, and even it received fewer votes than the special majority it has had in parliament that allowed it to continuously change the constitution to fit it to its narrow political interests. It is no wonder that many liberals are considering electoral reforms as parts of planned or imagined liberal restoration (Drutman 2020). Proportional representation is most democratic because it simply represents the distribution of votes. In Italy and Israel it did not prevent the emergence of neo-illiberal and populist coalition governments, but they have been less stable and easier to replace because new coalitions may emerge without the illiberal party as in Italy, and elections may replace an illiberal government that cannot gerrymander the results.

Two rounds of elections allow voters to vote idealistically in the first round and strategically in the second round. When voters vote for the lesser evil candidate in the second round, the more centrist candidate tends to have a broader appeal than an extremist. For example, in France and in Austria the more centrist candidates for president, Macron and Van der Bellen, defeated the populist neo-illiberal Le Pen and Hofer. Two electoral rounds are not panaceas. For example, Czech neo-illiberal populist president Zeman, defeated in the second round a centrist apolitical candidate and a former head of the Czech Academy of Science. But two rounds reduce the odds of an illiberal result.

Even better, in the *alternative vote* (also called *instant runoff*) method of election, voters rank candidates in order of preference. If no candidate wins an outright majority, the least popular candidate's votes go to the second preferences on the ballots, and so on until a candidate achieves a majority. Alternative vote systems are practiced in parliamentary elections in Australia and for presidential elections in Ireland. Such systems favor centrist candidates because though the first choices may be extreme, the second and third choices that would win the largest number of votes are likely to be more centrist. Alternative vote further makes party primaries redundant, as they are included in the general elections, since more than one candidate from each party may stand for elections for each seat or office. When political parties have small and shrinking memberships due to general alienation because of elitist democratic politics, neo-illiberal or populist, or simply deeply committed activists who may be extremists, who are better mobilized, motivated, and engaged, can dominate the results of primaries that do not represent the preferences of the population at large. In alternative vote systems, several candidates of the same political party may run for the same offices. So, in this primary rolled into general election, the general electorate may dilute the extremist vote.

The usefulness of plebiscites as a populist and totalitarian tool that leads to illiberal results by over-simplifying questions, limiting choice to simple "yes" or "no" options, and manipulating the political passions, has been recognized, at least since the tribunes of the Plebs who invented it, Napoleon who used it, and their frequent use by interwar Fascists. After Brexit and the failure of Renzi's plebiscite in Italy, it is unlikely that non-populist politicians will try them again to break a political stalemate; that would amount to carelessness, not just misfortune. But it would be even better consti-tutionally to take them off the political menu: prohibit plebiscites, at least on the national level. Democratic representatives are elected and paid to study and deal with complex issues and negotiate compromises. They should do their jobs.

New Liberalism without Nostalgia

I use here "new-liberalism" rather than "neoliber-alism" as the opposite alternative to neo-illiberalism. "Neoliberalism" has been conceptually abused and deformed from left and right. "Neoliberalism" has been misused, by both its defenders and detractors, to refer to the exact opposite of its literal meaning, to bad central planning, government intrusion, and a particular type of bureaucratic populism. It became associated with a school of public administration self-identified as "new public management," that promised to achieve what Communism could not have delivered, top-down scien-tific-technocratic planned solutions to policy problems. It advocated investing powers with consumer-friendly public managers and planners. At the heart of this approach lies a false analogy, more like a metaphor, between public service entitlements and their beneficiaries and private firms and their customers. Without a pricing mechanism and market regulations, new public management tries to *"simulate"* markets by analogy or metaphor, much like Soviet central planners.

Making "customers" happy, satisfying their passions, by empowering "managers" who are not accountable to shareholders or owners, leads to satisfying short-term passions rather than long-term interests: Prescribing opioids to addicts at the expense of the tax payer will make the addicts "satisfied," the managers "successful," and the service cheap and efficient, except that it is neither in the public interest, nor in any liberal tradition. Opiates to the masses was a Marxian description of religion, not a liberal government program. Similarly, "bureaucratic populists" can satisfy the passions of parents and their children by giving everybody a university degree with good grades. The new public managers are happy to accommodate. So, they provide mass, low quality, undemanding education, which does not give students the difficult skills they need to acquire but instead gives them beautiful large gold-rimmed degree diplomas that proud parents can hang above the kid's bed at home, because this is where their child will go on living for a while. The unintended result of new public management of education has been further devaluation of the value of state-public education and further exit for private education (Tucker 2015, 190–203; Muller 2018, 67–101).

New public management resorted to pseudo-scientific methods that made problems worse by ridiculously mismeasuring wrong, and sometimes diametrically opposite, indicators. For example, by using the satisfaction of patients to mismeasure the quality of medical care, they measured and consequently encouraged the prescription of opioids. By mismeasuring the effectiveness of teachers by the grades they give to their students, they encouraged the teachers to cheat on their students' exams and inflate their grades, thus measuring dishonesty rather than quality teaching. By mismeasuring the quality of universities by their retention rates, they measured and consequently encouraged them to dumb down their requirements and inflate their grades. By mismeasuring the success of surgeons and hospitals according to the survival rate of patients, they encouraged the best or most powerful doctors and hospitals to reject patients with difficult conditions that have low chances of survival or recovery, exactly the kind of patients who could use the best hospitals and doctors, and so on. (See the many excellent examples for the mismeasurement of all things in Muller 2018.)

Liberalism in any real sense wants governments to be small, efficient, effective, and well constrained by independent institutions and civil society. The application of the "neoliberal" label to its bureaucratic opposite intended to confuse and bewilder by obfuscation. If people who oppose bureaucratic populism come to believe this was "neoliberalism," then it has no radical alternative because the linguistic opposite of liberalism is central planning, and neoliberalism has come to mean central planning; George Orwell would have celebrated. To avoid further confusions then, I use "New Liberalism."

A standard new theoretical interpretation of the political polarization of the second decade of the twenty-first century argues convincingly that the distinctions between left and right have become obsolete. The new relevant political distinctions are between globalists and nativists, between supporters of open and closed societies, or between people from "nowhere" and people from "somewhere." But the exclusively bivalent choices between globalism and nativism, nowhere and somewhere, humanity and nationality or locality, make false assumptions. De Maistre at the dawn of the liberal era famously opined that "there is no such thing as 'man' in this world. In my life I have seen Frenchmen, Italians, Russians, and so on. I even know, thanks to Montesquieu, that one can be Persian. But as for man, I declare I've never encountered him" (de Maistre 1994). In my own life I have never encountered "the Frenchman" or "the Italian" either. I have seen and encountered people, individuals, who were different from each other. Some considered themselves French and Italian. Few spoke Persian and many liked Russian literature. People may be from several, non-mutually-exclusive places, feel at home in Paris and Venice and dream of St. Petersburg, while hoping to return to Persia after it is liberated from theocracy. People may and often do combine cultures and travel between them. The result is *syncretic*; it fuses, combines, and reconciles different cultures, beliefs, norms and habits. Syncretism is not multi-cultural in the sense of having several distinct identities co-existing, but of having vaguely and ambiguously defined cultures and identities interact to create hybrid versions, fuse, converse, exchange, and so on, to multiply and create together myriad other individual cultures, rather than homogenize. The global big cities that are the bastions of new liberalism are already largely syncretic in this sense.

It is natural to look for analogies between our era and the previous era of globalization that came to a crushing and violent end with the First World War. But the political basis of that globalization was not liberal-democratic, but imperialist and colonial. Labor mobility had a single direction, from the colonial centers to the colonies. Few European empires managed globalization, largely by coercion. Consequently, when Europe set about to destroy itself in an explosion of populist authoritarianism, the trade routes that passed through Europe and between European empires were destroyed. Imperial trade and labor mobility declined once former colonies became independent.

By contrast, contemporary globalization does not depend on imperialism or colonialism. It is multi-polar with a strong Asian and American (North and South) poles. This time it is different because even if Europe tears itself apart yet again, and the United States surrounds itself with walls and tariffs, globalization will continue in other, more populous, parts of the world. New information and communication technologies that made geographical, social, and political distances irrelevant for communication and information transmission are not going to disappear because of neo-illiberalism and populism. There is no "Suez Canal" or "Melaka Straits" in cyber space. Other innovations that are not likely to disappear, like cheap international travel, mobile phones, GPS, and digital social networks, will continue to reduce the cost of migration, irrespective of ancient low-tech barriers to mobility that were not effective, even for Hadrian's Rome and China's Ming Dynasty. The physical alternative is the construction of a new militarized iron curtain, with all its human and economic costs. Such a barrier would still not prevent people from exchanging information freely, irrespective of distance. Global travel would remain cheap. Though global trade can be made more difficult, it cannot be stopped altogether.

The appropriate analogy, then, is not so much with nineteenth-century globalization, as with the Hellenic and Roman globalizations. The expansion of the Macedonian empire and later the Roman Empire around the Mediterranean and into Europe, Asia, and Africa allowed free trade, mobility, and exchanges of cultures and genes between very different people. The Roman Empire leveled geopolitical and cultural barriers and left only natural barriers – the Sahara desert to the South, the Hindu-Kush Mountains to the East, the Atlantic to the West, and impenetrable forests and cold seas to the North. Rome gradually expanded the scope of Roman citizenship that granted rights that were the closest though still distant ancient approximation to rights in their modern liberal sense, till finally in 212 Emperor Caracalla's *Constitutio Antoniniana* granted universal citizenship to everybody. The empire facilitated religious, cultural, and artistic syncretism, ethnic hybridization, and trade globalization. Within this space, cosmopolitan ideals manifested themselves most clearly in the elite's Roman law and Stoic philosophy. But Roman identity expanded by creating *syncretic* more than *universal* identities. The most famous product and vehicle for the distribution of this syncretism that lasts to this day is Christianity, the worship of a universal globalist and cosmopolitan abstract God by a syncretic collection of beliefs, myths, and rituals from around the ancient Mediterranean. Many other syncretic alternatives to Christianity and other versions of Christianity co-existed for centuries before political Caesaro-Papism forced homogenization. The process of syncretization took place in the great cities of the Roman Empire from Rome to Antioch and between.

Similarly today, the work of syncretization takes place in the great cities. Syncretization is neither immigrant assimilation to a homogenous population (for example the total assimilation of Czechs who settled in Vienna during the nineteenth century within a generation, or of immigrants to the United States within a generation or two), nor common assimilation of all native cultures into a general universal commercial vulgarity, that Europeans like to misidentify with Walt Disney. This Hellenic or Roman syncretization and expansion of citizenship and rights may define a new cultural liberalism, in addition to strengthening the barriers to absolutism and preempting the self-destructive passions of populism. Within a political space of cultural and economic syncretism, new political forms may emerge by distinguishing territoriality and sovereignty from political affiliation. Citizens of many non-territorial states that serve their citizens according to contracts, irrespective of their geographic location, like insurance companies, may intermingle and interact in great cities (Tucker and de Bellis 2016; MacDonald 2019).

The moment for new liberalism may arrive unannounced, as the moment for old liberalism came following the collapse of Communism in 1989. The geopolitical and soft powers of the United States are still so overwhelming that if a liberal democrat wins the American elections, for example by defeating Trump in the 2020 presidential elections, this victory will marginalize neo-illiberals everywhere and generate liberal contagion. A successful liberal presidency will restore the soft power of liberalism and neo-illiberal democracies will implode as the Soviet Empire did, from within, though a little help from outside will not hurt either.

If the neo-illiberal slide is halted in good time with a landslide victory of a liberal-democratic president who understands and cares for the world, the United States may once again step in to the rescue of the old world and liberate it from its own neo-illiberalism. In the meanwhile, we must ride out the populist storm to outlive the menace of illiberalism, and plan for restored, yet new, liberal sunlit syncretic uplands.

References

Albright, Madeleine (2018) *Fascism: A Warning*. New York: Harper.

Baldwin, Richard (2016) *The Great Convergence: Information Technology and the New Globalization*. Cambridge: Harvard University Press.

Ben–Menahem, Yemima (1997) "Historical Contingency," *Ratio* 10 (2), 99–107.

Canovan, Margaret (2005) *The People*. Cambridge: Polity.

Chatterji, Angana P., Hansen, Thomas Blom, and Jaffrelot, Christophe eds. (2019) *The Majoritarian State: How Hindu Nationalism is Changing India*. London: Hurst and Co.

De Maistre, Joseph (1994) *Considerations on France*. Trans. Richard Lebrun. Cambridge: Cambridge University Press.

Drutman, Lee (2020) *Breaking the Two-Party Doom Loop*. New York: Oxford University Press.

Economist, the editors of (2019) "The Entanglement of Powers," *Economist*, August 31, 15–18.

Elster, Jon (1999) *Alchemies of the Mind: Rationality and the Emotions*. New York: Cambridge University Press.

Elster, Jon (2018) "The Resistible Rise of Louis Bonaparte," in Cass R. Sunstein ed., *Can It Happen Here? Authoritarianism in America*. New York: Dey Street, 277–312.

Fishkin, Joseph (2014) *Bottlenecks: A New Theory of Equal Opportunity*. New York: Oxford University Press.

Frankfurt, Harry G. (1988) *The Importance of What We Care About: Philosophical Essays*. Cambridge: Cambridge University Press.

Ginsburg, Tom and Huq, Aziz Z. (2018) *How to Save a Constitutional Democracy*. Chicago: University of Chicago Press.

Guest, Robert (2011) *Borderless Economics: Chinese Sea Turtles, Indian Fridges and the New Fruits of Global Capitalism*. New York: St. Martin's Griffin.

Herf, Jeffrey (2016a) "Is Donald Trump a Fascist?" *The American Interest*, published online March 7, 2016.

Herf, Jeffrey (2016b) "Postscript to is Donald Trump a Fascist?" *The American Interest*, published online August 8, 2016.

Holmes, Stephen (1995) *Passions and Constraints: On the Theory of Liberal Democracy*. Chicago: University of Chicago Press.

Holmes, Stephen (2018) "How Democracies Perish," in Cass R. Sunstein ed., *Can It Happen Here? Authoritarianism in America*. New York: Dey Street, 387–428.

Inkpen, Rob and Turner, Derek (2012) "The Topography of Historical Contingency," *Journal of the Philosophy of History* 6 (1), 1–19.

Kershaw, Ian (2015) *To Hell and Back: Europe 1914–1949*. London: Allen Lane.

Levitsky, Steven and Way, Lucan (2010) *Competitive Authoritarianism: Hybrid Regimes after the Cold War*. New York: Cambridge University Press.

Levitsky, Steven and Ziblatt, Daniel (2018) *How Democracies Die*. New York: Crown.

MacDonald, Trent J. (2019) *The Political Economy of Non-Territorial Exit*. Cheltenham: Edward Elgar.

Magyar, Bálint (2016) *Post-Communist Mafia State: The Case of Hungary*. Budapest: Central European University Press.

Mitchell, Thomas N. (2015) *Democracy's Beginning: The Athenian Story*. New Haven: Yale University Press.

Mounk, Yascha (2018) *The People vs. Democracy: Why Our Freedom is in Danger and How to Save It*. Cambridge MA: Harvard University Press.

Müller, Jan-Werner (2016) *What is Populism?* Philadelphia: University of Pennsylvania Press.

Muller, Jerry Z. (2018) *The Tyranny of Metrics*. Princeton: Princeton University Press.

Murray, Charles (2012) *Coming Apart: The State of White America 1960–2010*. New York: Crown Forums.

Niklewicz, Konrad (2017) "Taming the Beast," *Aspen Review Central Europe* 1, 16–21.

Norris, Pippa and Inglehart, Ronald (2019) *Cultural Backlash: Trump, Brexit, and Authoritarian Populism*. New York: Cambridge University Press.

Ober, Josiah (1989) *Mass and Elite in Democratic Athens: Rhetoric Ideology, and the Power of the People*. Princeton: Princeton University Press.

Pinker, Steven (2012) *The Better Angels of our Nature: Why Violence has Declined*. New York: Penguin Books.

Pinker, Steven (2018) *Enlightenment Now: The Case for Reason, Science, Humanism, and Progress*. New York: Viking.

Posner, Eric (2018) "The Dictator's Handbook, US Edition," in Cass R. Sunstein ed., *Can It Happen Here? Authoritarianism in America*. New York: Dey Street, 1–18.

Przeworski, Adam (1991) *Democracy and the Market*. New York: Cambridge University Press.

Przeworski, Adam (1995) *Sustainable Democracy*. New York: Cambridge University Press.

Przeworski, Adam, Alvarez, Michael E., Cheibub, Jose Antonio, and Limongi, Fernando (2000) *Democracy and Development: Political Institutions and Well-Being in the World, 1950–1990*. New York: Cambridge University Press.

Railton, Peter (1986) "Moral Realism," *The Philosophical Review* 95 (2), 163–207.

Rajah, Jothie (2012) *Authoritarian Rule of Law: Legislation, Discourse, and Legitimacy in Singapore*. Cambridge: Cambridge University Press.

Reeves, Richard V. (2017) *Dream Hoarders: How the American Upper Middle Class is Leaving Everyone Else in the Dust, Why That is a Problem and What to do About It*. Washington DC: Brookings Institute.

Runciman, David (2018) *How Democracy Dies*. London: Profile Books.

Samons II, Loren J. (2004) *What's Wrong with Democracy? From Athenian Practice to American Worship*. Berkeley: University of California Press.

Sartori, Giovanni (1987) *The Theory of Democracy Revisited*. Chatham NJ: Chatham House.

Signer, Michael (2009) *Demagogue: The Fight to Save Democracy from its Worst Enemies*. New York: Palgrave-Macmillan.

Snyder, Timothy (2017) *On Tyranny: Twenty Lessons from the Twentieth Century*. New York: Tim Duggan.

Sridharan, E. (2017) "Middle Class Votes for BJP," in *Electoral Politics in India: The Resurgence of the Bharatiya Janata Party*, Suhas Palshikar et al. eds., Abingdon: Routledge, 270–281.

Stenner, Karen and Haidt, Jonathan (2018) "Authoritarianism is not a momentary madness, but an eternal dynamics within liberal democracies," in Cass R. Sunstein ed., *Can It Happen Here? Authoritarianism in America*. New York: Dey Street, 175–220.

Sterelny, Kim (2016) "Contingency and History," *Philosophy of Science* 83 (4), 521–539.

Stockemer, Daniel, Lentz, Tobias, and Mayer, Danielle (2018) "Individual Predictors of the Radical Right-Wing Vote in Europe: A Meta-Analysis of Articles in Peer-Reviewed Journals (1995–2016)" *Government and Opposition* 53 (3), 569–593.

Thucydides (2009) *The Peloponnesian War.* Trans. Martin Hammond. Oxford: Oxford University Press.

Tucker, Aviezer (2004) *Our Knowledge of the Past: A Philosophy of Historiography.* New York: Cambridge University Press.

Tucker, Aviezer (2015) *The Legacies of Totalitarianism: A Theoretical Framework.* New York: Cambridge University Press.

Tucker, Aviezer (2016) "The Generation of Knowledge from Multiple Testimonies," *Social Epistemology* 30, 251–272.

Tucker, Aviezer (2017) "Fifty Shades of Czech Populism," *The American Interest*, October 23, 2017.

Tucker, Aviezer (2019a) "Universal Basic Income: Does It Work," *The American Interest*, June 12, 2019.

Tucker, Aviezer (2019b) "Otevřený dopis Jiřímu Drahošovi k situaci v Ústavu pro studium totalitních režimů/Open Letter to Senator Drahoš about the Situation in the Institute for Study of Totalitarian Regimes," *Bubínek Revolveru*, published online August 5, 2019.

Tucker, Aviezer and De Bellis, Gian Piero eds. (2016) *Panarchy: Political Theories of Non-Territorial States*, New York: Routledge.

Zakaria, Fareed (2003) *The Future of Freedom: Illiberal Democracy at Home and Abroad.* New York: Norton.

Index